## An Attorney Shows You How To

# PLAN YOUR ESTATE

by

George Hardisty
Attorney at Law

with

Margaret Hardisty

**Carodyn Publishers**
Lafayette, California

S0-BPO-792

# An Attorney Shows You How To Plan Your Estate

Copyright © 1983 by George and Margaret Hardisty

*First Printing 1983*
*Second Printing 1984*

**Published by Carodyn Publishers**

ISBN 0-913143-00-6
Library of Congress Catalog Card No. 83-71707

**Cataloging in Publication Data**

Hardisty, George

Plan your estate, an attorney shows you how to

1. Estate planning—United States. I. Hardisty, Margaret, joint author. II. Title.

KF750.H365        346'.73'052
ISBN-0-913143-00-6                              83-71707

Unless otherwise identified, Scripture quotations are based on the King James Version of the Bible.

Scripture quotation on page 180 is from The Living Bible, Copyright © 1971 by Tyndale House Publishers, Wheaton, Illinois 60187. All rights reserved.

"For You" by Martha Snell Nicholson. Moody Press, Moody Bible Institute of Chicago. Used by permission.

Excerpt from *George Mueller, Man of Faith* Ed. by A. Sims, Copyright 1958. Moody Press, Moody Bible Institute of Chicago. Used by permission.

Joke which appears on page 110 is taken from *The World's Greatest Collection of Clean Jokes,* by Bob Phillips, p. 122, copyright 1974, Vision House Publishers, Ventura, California. Used by permission. All rights reserved.

Illustrations by Robert Badaracco
Cover by Colleen Dossey

*Printed in the United States of America*

*Dedicated to the memory of Lauretta M. Walkup, George's mother, who was an immeasurable inspiration and encouragement to both of us.*

By George and Margaret Hardisty
  *Honest Questions, Honest Answers*
  *Successful Financial Planning*
  *How to Enrich Your Marriage*

By Margaret Hardisty
  *Forever My Love*
  *Your Husband and Your Emotional Needs*

# Contents

# Preface

One friend and client wrote, "The book you are writing, in my estimation, will be received by many grateful hearts. To the average person, such words as Probate, Estate Taxes, Inheritance Taxes, Trusts, Codicils, Annuities, etc., are simply words with strange meanings. Because people are expected to know—but don't—their pride keeps them from asking, in order to understand. We had a seminar just recently, and even though people sat listening attentively, afterward, privately, so many confessed that they were lost after the first five minutes."

That's one of the reasons why I asked Margaret to coauthor this book with me. She said, "Law confuses me. If we write this so *I* can understand *everything* you are saying, *anyone* will be able to grasp it."

We spent many hours huddled over terms or statements I had written in the book, until they were clear to her. Then she rewrote many of those in lay language.

The result, we trust, is a helpful tool for the layperson, to give you a workable, informative knowledge of many points of law regarding estate planning. Furthermore, we hope that by the time you have finished this book, you will be acquainted with most of the terms that have overwhelmed you in the past when you have heard them used by the professional.

The questions people ask across the country are surprisingly similar, but in searching for answers to some of your questions, as you read, keep in mind that the laws of the fifty states differ in many areas. Not only that, the laws are constantly changing, so that today's answer may be different tomorrow. As a result, our answers are general in nature, with little consideration for possible exceptions.

The purpose of this book, then, is not to offer a substitute for local professional advice. Indeed, we would hope that it will motivate you to seek out that advice in order to keep your legal and financial affairs as clear of trouble as possible, help you use the law to your advantage rather than to your disadvantage, and assist you and your counsel in completing your own tailor-made estate plan.

Furthermore, all cases presented herein are either a conglomeration of several actual cases, or are fictitious in whole or part to illustrate a point. All names have been changed, and all facts are presented so as to protect completely all clients and keep their confidence.

GEORGE HARDISTY

# Acknowledgments

To the hundreds of persons from across the nation, among whom are attorneys, stewardship representatives, accountants, investment counselors, pastors, insurance men, trustees, and laypeople who took the time to answer our request for questions from their experience, we give a special thanks. Your response was overwhelming and gratifying, and many of your questions are included in this book.

One attorney friend, Sunshine Summers, not only sent a written list of questions he has been asked over the years, as he has represented one of the nation's finest universities and other clients, but he prepared and sent a tape which verbalized not only questions, but the answers to those questions as well! John G. Watts, Planned Giving Director of Navigators, took the time to prepare and send pages of questions which people have asked him during the great number of seminars on estate planning he has conducted across the country. These are just examples of many others who responded the same way.

We had the privilege of submitting a copy of the manuscript for review and suggestions to Marvin E. Beckman, attorney at law of Chicago, Illinois; Phillip T. Temple, attorney at law of New York, New York; William T. Eckhoff and John H. Rolling, Certified Public Accountants of San Rafael, California; Roger L. Minor, attorney at law of Torrance, California; and two of my law partners: Robert H. Peterson of San Francisco, California, and Edward E. Barr of Lafayette, California. Their suggestions and counsel have been of great help.

The unselfishness and encouragement which all of you have given in letters, by phone, and in person have been a mainstay in these months of day-and-night effort to produce a useful tool for the layperson.

For further and in-depth study of many of the areas of law we include, we recommend the books on the various subjects as listed in our Bibliography.

**Chapter 1**

# *Harnessing Your Assets*

Harnessing all those assets so they are working FOR you can be fun. Exhilarating! The miseries start when they begin working AGAINST you.

Our daughter and son once bought a horse. That horse was begging to be brought home! He nuzzled and snuggled up to every one of us to show what a regular guy he was. We were astounded that he was so perfect, since he didn't cost but a pittance.

We should have gotten a clue when the former owner delivered him and volunteered, "It took me an hour to get him into the trailer."

But it didn't register. We were anxious to introduce him to his new home. And he liked it! In fact, he claimed it as his own immediately. He trotted around the corral, testing the strength of the fence, stomping on the bushes we had planted there for decorative purposes, and kicking his water tub.

The next clue came when the kids decided to saddle him up for the first historic ride. Much to their surprise, however, he didn't WANT to be saddled up and by the time he WAS, they were exhausted and decided to take a rest instead.

When the ride finally took place, it was, indeed, historic—at least, for our family. That horse imagined every leaf and stick to be a dragon of the fiercest type which must be avoided at all costs by leaping from side to side.

And then, just a half mile up the road, he decided to go home. Suddenly, he reared straight up in the air, got rid of the burden on his back, and hightailed it right back to where the oats were.

Although he's been blessing another owner for a long time now, he's still got our offspring fooled. They insist that we're exaggerating and it wasn't the poor horse's fault, anyhow, and besides, if they'd had more TIME, they could have controlled him.

Undoubtedly they could have, after a few broken bones and disfigured faces. Personally, I'm glad to be rid of him. It's no fun losing control of something that should be controlled by you.

Just as one can lose control of a horse, so he can lose control of his assets. They begin to control him, instead! And, in fact, if he doesn't realize his mistake soon enough, the ornery critters can gallop right off and get out of sight altogether.

Sometimes those runaway assets can never be found, corralled, and used again. But once you've got your hands on them, or on new ones that come your way, the trick is to keep them where you want them at all times. And the best way I know how to do that is to have some sort of plan.

The reason our horse got the upper hoof (uh—hand) was that he had it all planned out before we ever got there. He knew exactly what he was going to do. He also knew that we DIDN'T know what we were going to do. We didn't have a PLAN. He did.

So it is with financial success. To keep trouble from knocking your financial door down or from torturing your loved ones after you have left this earthly scene, we suggest that you:

## Set Some Goals

What do you want out of life? Buy a home? Build up a savings account? Be sure your family is well cared for? Travel to a faraway, exotic place where they don't have horses? Make your list of dreams and then set about making some or all of them come true. The logical question at this point is,

### *How do I start making them come true?*

Start by becoming *knowledgeable!*

## It Happened One Friday Night

Two hundred and fifty people crowded the room for the estate planning meeting. Ted was there, hoping to get some guidance before joining three of his buddies in a $3,000,000 apartment complex investment. He had brought his neighbor, Mrs. Barry, along. She was confused about her finances and had been since her husband died.

Ben and Judy had come. Ben's response to Judy when she told him about the meeting had been "Anything! Anything that'll help us get out of this mess we're in. Overdue bills! That's all I see anymore."

And sitting just in back of them were the Blakemores who had arrived with their teenagers. Jim was anxious for Dolly and the children to learn everything they could about estate planning in case his bad heart decided to call it quits.

The speakers on the program included an investment broker, an accountant, and an attorney. Their respective talks were interesting and informative, as was the film that followed.

At the coffee break, Judy bubbled, "This has been fantastic! They've even talked about how we can get some of those things I've been wanting for so long—a trip around the world, a mansion . . . . "

"Don't we wish," Ben laughed. "But I *can* see ways now how we can save, cut costs, and realize some dreams we never thought possible."

The Blakemores had stayed seated. Dolly squeezed Jim's hand. Their son brought them coffee and said, with tears in his eyes, "Dad, nothing's going to happen to you. I just know it."

His dad smiled, "I agree, son. Fact is, I'll probably outlive you!" And then he turned serious. "But just in case, I want to be sure everything is in order."

Still at the table, Mrs. Barry reached for a cookie. "You know, Ted, I didn't realize how important it was for me to have a will. I would hate to have most of my money fall into the wrong hands. And I was surprised at all the taxes one can save. My church needs it a whole lot more than the government. And maybe, just maybe, it *would* be wise for me to join you in investing in that apartment complex."

"Well," Ted answered, "before either of us decides anything, Mrs. Barry, we've got to get someone to help us who knows more about these things than we do."

Later, when the seminar was over, Ben and Judy made their way to the front and asked to speak with the investment broker. "You'll think I'm pretty stupid, I suppose," Ben started his conversation. "I don't have any money at all, and I'm in debt. I just wondered if maybe you could show me how all this I heard tonight could apply to my case."

The broker smiled, "I've heard this story before, Ben. But, as the film said, you probably have more than you think, and, in any event, we can show you ways to get ahead."

The following week, in the broker's office, Ben saw that

it was true. He did have more than he thought.

"Ben, you make enough money so that you should be able, eventually, to get that little home you've always dreamed about, and have a few small investments on the side, as well. We'll have to set out a budget for you to follow, though, so your money doesn't keep slipping through your fingers."

Within a short time, the budget was outlined, and Ben saw new hope for the future. "But why insurance?" he asked. "That's costly."

"Because," the broker said, "if you get the right plan, your estate will be worth a whole lot more than it is now, should you die, say, next week. You need that protection for your wife and children. Look, I have the names of several insurance men here. Go to one of them, and let him show you the different options available. He'll probably want you to work with an attorney who knows his business, too, and you can coordinate your insurance with a will."

Ben gulped, "Will? How much does that cost?"

"It's not what it costs. It's what it will cost if you

DON'T have one that's important. You should see what
happens to your assets when you die without a will! And if
both you and Judy should die, without one, your little kids
may have a rough life ahead of them.''

Maybe you'll want to attend a meeting similar to the one
we described. They are often sponsored by a religious or civic
group. If so, you may want an answer to this question:

### *Do I pay for these meetings?*

Sometimes. Sometimes not. Generally, each organization
which does *not* charge has an ulterior motive besides the
desire to help you. They either want to sell you their services
or their product, or they are hoping you will share your assets
with them, either now, or after your death, so their work can
continue. Their motives shouldn't stop you, for you have no
obligation to them. Pressures generally are not brought to
bear on you at all, and you can learn much in the process. It
has been my privilege to speak at many such seminars.

Some seminars are moneymaking ventures for those who
conduct them and you pay for the privilege of listening to
their advice, but you are apprised of this before you decide to
participate.

### Widows, Widows, Everywhere!

We want you to notice that Jim, who attended the seminar
we described, was not only wise in deciding to plan his future,
but was doubly wise in insisting that Dolly and the children be
knowledgeable in all aspects of it.

Facts aren't always pleasant, but we have to face up to
them sooner or later, and when it comes to life and death, it is
better to face up to them sooner. In March of 1980, according
to the United States Bureau of Census, there were 10,479,000
widows in this country, but only 1,972,000 widowers.
Women, at the time of this writing, are expected to live seven
to eight years longer than their husbands. If you are married,
it is vital for you and your spouse to work together in all matters regarding family business, for the wife is likely to be a
widow someday and forced to handle matters by herself.

## Valuable Advice

The old pastor had been so wise. In the premarital counseling sessions he'd had with Dick and Shirley, he pointed out to them that, even though they were the same age, Shirley was expected to live longer than Dick. He told them they should begin their marriage preparing Shirley for widowhood. He shared with them what fun it had been for him and his wife, over the years, to plan, build, and do together many things that other couples thought unnecessary. And part of that doing together was making provisions for when they must part.

So Dick and Shirley did their planning. They budgeted, dreamed, and set goals—together. This they continued after they married. Dick shared business matters with Shirley and encouraged her to develop her own talents, not just live in his shadow. Shirley managed the house account and purchased as needed. She made some wise investments in areas where Dick, though interested, was too busy to search out thoroughly. Later, as children became part of their lives, they enjoyed holding family conferences to discuss any problems anyone had.

Dick and Shirley planned their estate and funded it so that she would never be in need. After the children completed their schooling, and Dick and Shirley retired, they shared a mutual interest in charity, travel, and the arts.

When Dick died, he left Shirley with many pleasant memories of their years together, and, now as a widow, she had worry-free times ahead, capable in her own right of carrying on the things she and Dick started, ably assisted by an attorney, a tax consultant, and her pastor—all men whom she and Dick had come to know and work with in the past.

## Then There Were Rory and Alice

Rory worked hard for his money and made it known to the fellows that the way to run a house was to keep the little woman " . . . barefoot and pregnant!" He earned the money, and so he figured he had a right to spend it—any way he wished. He invested as he thought wise, added to his benefits at work—or dropped them—as he thought best. He pushed papers in front of Alice with one word of advice, "Sign."

One evening, on the way home from a night out with "the boys," Rory was killed in an auto accident. Imagine the shock to Alice as she drifted through the funeral in a haze. What would she do with her life and their four children? She had no idea if they had any property besides their home. She had heard Rory mention an investment he was considering in Texas. Had he gone ahead with it? She wasn't sure what they owed or to whom, nor did she know where Rory kept their papers.

So the nightmare began; a nightmare which eventually would be worked out, but after much trouble and cost. Because Rory had not consulted anyone, and much of his management had been foolish, Alice had to go back to work, leaving the three youngest children in the care of a sitter, and she has had to fight a feeling of resentment toward Rory and her memories of him.

### It's Not Always the Husband's Fault

Many widows have confessed to me that their husbands had tried many times and in different ways to interest them in matters of finances as the children were growing, and later, when they were alone in retirement, but that they were just not interested. That, after all, was where husbands' interests were, they reasoned, and as one woman said, "I was too busy with other things that interested me. Now that he's gone, I just don't know what I'm going to do."

Taking the time and effort to be involved in your family partnership in the area of finances, ladies, will work to cement and make more solid your whole marriage relationship, whether you are a bride of six months or thirty-five years.

### But Then Again

Maybe you are ready now to become more knowledgeable about how to realize your goals and dreams, but perhaps attending a seminar isn't to your liking. Books may be your thing. There are books on everything from how Mr. Aged discovered the secret of youth to how to outwit ornery horses. Some of them should stay in the bookstore. But when it comes to setting goals, making a budget, sticking to that budget, cutting costs, getting out of debt, and getting ahead financially, there are some very GOOD books available. That's one reason why we aren't going to go into that aspect of financial planning in this one. We have touched upon the subject in our previously published volumes, *Honest Questions, Honest Answers* and *How to Enrich Your Marriage.* That and other works which will be of help to you are listed in the Bibliography.

**On the Other Hand**

Very little has been written for the layperson on the sometimes hard-to-understand processes of the law that affect the financial part of his or her life or the lives of loved ones after he or she is gone. Therefore, this book will concentrate primarily on that emphasis.

**It's Time to Move On**

Whether you attend a seminar, read books, or whatever, when you realize what needs to be done to reasonably assure a safe future for you and your loved ones, your next step will be to see a professional in the field, one we call an *Estate Planning Specialist.* A specialist can analyze your problem and prepare a plan to serve you best, in a lot less time than the novice. So let's consider what experts are available in this field.

# Chapter 2

# *What's an Expert?*

As the old saying goes: X is an unknown quantity. Spurt is a drip under pressure. That is one definition of an "expert."

> Dan was all personality and shiny teeth. He spoke with confidence. There wasn't anything he couldn't fix on a car or truck! To prove it, he offered to make a friend's automobile " . . . like new!" I was happy to lend my electric drill and other tools to such a capable fellow.
>
> "I'll have it done in a week," he shouted back to us as he strode purposefully away.
>
> Four weeks later, our friend's car still sat unfixed. The tools I needed had not been returned as promised. And to top it all off, the neighbors informed us that Dan's own van, on which he had worked extensively, blew up! It caught on fire! It totaled itself! We haven't seen the car "expert" since.

Unfortunately, the designation, Estate Planning Specialist, is rather loosely used by various persons both in and out of the legal profession.

> *"So how am I to know?" Barry asked. "And to whom should I go?"*

Be wary of the person who has some special interest to sell or promote and pushes the do-it-yourself course to the exclusion of a lawyer. The law doesn't prevent your doing it yourself, but the salesman or promoter who wants to avoid the scrutiny of a lawyer is suspect. Only a lawyer is licensed to practice law on your behalf. Anyone who practices law

without a license is breaking the law. You may feel that's one-sided, but the system we live in is set up that way and generally works for your protection and in your best interest.

## The Satisfied Customer

Nothing beats the recommendation of the satisfied customer. Since this is my field, I'm regularly asked to recommend estate planning specialists in other areas. If it's in a city across the country where I don't know anyone, I call the chairman of the Christian Businessmen's Committee in that town or an officer in some other organization whom I respect and trust. Often a friend or relative, a pastor, insurance man, accountant, or bank trust officer will have the names of men who have proven their expertise and who are honest. In other words, I find them by asking satisfied customers. You can, too.

## Colleges and Charities

*I give to my college and several of my favorite charities. They all send me information to aid*

*me with my estate planning and offer to send a
man to help me if I return a card asking for
him. Should I return the card?*

Most stewardship representatives are motivated to serve,
and although they are employed by one or, in some cases,
several organizations, and they hope you will remember those
organizations financially, they make it clear that the choice as
to whom you will give is yours alone. Most of them will help
you organize your assets and ideas and put you in touch with
several competent estate-planning attorneys from whom you
can choose.

I've been very grateful for these stewardship people. Their
preliminary work involving fact-finding often saves me hours
of time and thus saves money for my clients.

## Churches

*How can a church be helpful to people in the
area of wills and estate planning? What involvement should a pastor have in this area?*

One church sponsored a series of weekly one-hour
meetings held in the evening over a period of four weeks. An
accountant appeared the first week, an investment counselor
the next session. He was followed by a mortician, and on the
fourth week, I came, representing the legal profession. After
each short presentation, the meetings were open to questions,
answers, and discussion. The people were delighted with the
results.

## Insurance Men

*My life insurance agent says he is an estate
planner and wants to help me with my estate.
Should I let him?*

I know a number of insurance men who are excellent estate
planners. They have served hundreds of satisfied customers.
If you have one that meets our tests, then by all means, accept
his offer of help.

## Banks

> *My banker has offered the services of his Trust Department to help us with our estate planning. Are banks a good place to go for help?*

Yes, they can aid you in getting your estate property in order, can give you ideas to consider, and can refer you to competent legal counsel. Don't forget our "satisfied customer" test. It will work here, too.

## Lawyers

> *Any lawyer will do. Right?*

Wrong. You should be represented by a lawyer who *specializes* in this field. Estate planning, if properly done, involves more than the preparation of a will. Many lawyers who have not made this their specialty are not up to date on the latest rules and laws and often are confused by them.

Estate planning starts right where your need is.

One lady who came to me owns a home in a part of a city which is no longer the quiet, safe neighborhood it used to be. Her son and his family live in a cottage on the same property which the family had built some years before. The location was perfect for the son, for his work was nearby.

She sighed, "Oh, I wish I could move to the beautiful mobile park my cousin lives in. It's just what I've always dreamed of."

I looked at her for a moment and then asked, "Why don't you do it?"

She looked startled and then returned, "But that would be impossible. I have the responsibility of my present property, and except for the rent my son pays me, I have no other income." She thought for a moment. "Can you think of a way I could swing it?"

Before the hour was out, we had made plans for her to...

... sell the house and cottage to the son. Since commercial enterprises were starting to move into the neighborhood, he could sell later and make a profit. He was in a position to pay her a substantial down payment so she would have cash to use;

. . . buy in the mobile park where her cousin lived;

. . . use some of the excess money she would receive to take a trip to the Holy Land, one of her lifetime dreams.

What a new, exciting life is ahead for this widow!

## Those Days Are Gone Forever

I believe we are rapidly approaching the time when lawyers will be *schooled* and *licensed* to practice in specialized areas of the law. The days of the general practitioner are numbered and the day of the specialist is at hand. We see this in almost every field of endeavor: medicine, construction, electronics, and so on.

My first law partner started his practice shortly after World War I. Imagine my admiration of this well-respected man who not only practiced in most areas of the law, but had a real estate broker's license, sold insurance for several firms, and ran an electric motor repairing business on the side. Thus, I followed his leading and practiced general law for many years, but now I specialize in a few areas rather than many, and so do my law partners. Many attorneys have chosen this course so they can do the best possible job for their clientele.

Competent help is available and you can find it with a little effort on your part. But as you seek that help, remember some advice given in the world's Number One Best-Seller, the Holy Bible:

> Blessed is the man that walketh not in the counsel of the ungodly . . . .

If you find a competent professional who also loves the Lord, you have a winning combination. However, only God Himself truly knows the sincerity of a person's heart and the abilities that are built into that person. So even though the professional may be churchgoing and apparently devoted to spiritual matters, this does not assure competence in the field of estate planning. Here again, the recommendations of satisfied customers really help.

# Chapter 3

# *Attorneys Cost Too Much Money!*

It's a familiar cry, isn't it? And so is this one:

*Who needs professional help, anyhow? I've got everything under control.*

This came from the lips of a steel executive who thought he had everything in order through his company benefits office. Frankly, he was irritated at his wife, who had nagged him into coming in to see me. He had finally complied just to get her off his back. He didn't want to pay any attorney for telling him he had already done everything right.

So I agreed with his wife that if, after we had talked for an hour or so and I had gotten inside their thinking and affairs, it developed they needed or wanted no help from me, my total charge would be $35.00; and that would be the end of it.

It didn't take long to see that there was much he could learn. I showed him how $50,000 in taxes could be saved at his death by using an estate-splitting, tax-savings trust. He also was amazed at the savings that could be realized in probate fees by a change in his insurance beneficiary designation. Then what really got to him so that he practically jumped over my desk, was the revelation that, should he and his wife die with their present planning, his children might each receive over $100,000 in cash with no strings attached, at age eighteen, either to squander or spend wisely, and all he could think of was "squander." Thus we completed their planning which included making certain their children's lives wouldn't be ruined by receiving a sudden windfall.

Needless to say, they were extremely satisfied and never once mentioned my $35 pay-it-and-leave deal. (See Chapter 8, "Planning Ahead to Use Probate," for more on tax-savings trusts.)

**Rich Attorneys?**

The majority of attorneys I know aren't what you would call "rich," although most are in the upper-income bracket. Many attorneys make no more than top-salaried truck drivers these days. On top of it, they have secretaries to pay, rent to keep up, insurance, equipment, printing, traveling, and various other costs, as well as those of their own family and living expenses.

Your attorney may have more coming in than you, but he also may have more going out!

I don't believe most people can afford to be without an attorney. It is my contention that, in the long run, much more is saved by competent legal help than is spent. This is especially true in planning proper use of funds for the future and in connection with making a will.

One fellow shared with me later that, just as we began our first conference to handle his problems, he was thinking,

> *Why am I sitting here paying this guy for doing something I probably could do myself? How about those do-it-yourself forms? I should pick one up.*

He soon changed his mind, but I can identify with that kind of thinking. I would hate to have to call a carpenter when my front door needed fixing. I can do it myself! But, I have to admit, I'd be making a mistake if I tried to repair my television instead of calling a TV repairman.

**You Don't Have to Have a Lawyer**

There is no law that requires you to have a lawyer to assist you with a will or estate plan. You can prepare your own with or without the help of anyone. The law does require that

anyone who practices law on behalf of someone else *must* have a license to do so. If you prepare your own will and it contains everything it should to be legal and accomplish your purposes, then you're in good shape.

The *problem* lies in the law itself. Attorneys study continually to keep up with the law. They attend seminars periodically and receive literature which apprises them of new laws and rulings.

Our society becomes more complicated as time passes. I used to work on my Model A with a screwdriver and a pair of pliers. I don't dare get near the high-powered machinery of my present-day automobile. When I need a tooth filled, I go to a dentist. If I had a heart murmur, I would go to a doctor who is a heart specialist. When you draw up a will or complete an estate plan, you should go to a lawyer.

## How to Cut Costs

*Is there anything I can do to minimize the attorney's costs?*

Yes, when it comes to estate planning, data concerning you, your family, your estate, and your wishes must be compiled by the attorney before he can formulate your estate plan and that takes time for which he must charge. You can save most of that time by having all this prepared before you get to his office. Every stewardship department of organizations I have worked with over the years has forms they will give you to be used for this purpose. Many have representatives who will come to your home and help you if you need it. (See Chapter 6 for more on this.)

*How much is it going to cost me?*

Lawyers generally charge by the hour for this type of work. The hourly charge will vary from office to office and area to area. Because every case is different, and investigation sometimes unearths a Pandora's box of problems, it is unwise for any attorney to quote a total fee, unless it is for a very minimal will.

Some charge a flat initial conference fee and some charge according to the time spent in the first conference. At the end of that first conference, the counselor will be able to advise you of the total cost, in most instances. If you decide not to proceed, all you are out is the initial fee.

### Ask Him

Since there are various and sundry methods attorneys use to charge clients, it is well to ask your attorney right away *how* he will tabulate his fee, and reach an agreement right from the beginning.

With regard to the cost of estate work after a client dies, it isn't fair to you or those who will work for you, to have me or anyone else pull a percentage out of the air and say it will be two percent or seven, or twelve percent of your estate. The fee will ordinarily be larger for a big estate, but not always. If your plan provides a way for the property to pass on to others without probate or extensive service, the fee on a huge estate could be a pittance. (See Chapters 10 through 13 on how to avoid probate.)

**There Are Safeguards**

Although there are several methods of determining fees for estate work, as listed below, the way it is done in your state may be different from others.

The attorney and executor fees are either:

1. Set by the legislature, computed on the amount of the estate;
2. Fixed as a percentage of the estate based on a local fee schedule; or
3. Based upon the reasonable value of services rendered.

Subject to restrictions in the local law, the fees to be charged may be agreed upon in advance by the parties.

In a court-supervised trust, the trustee's fee is determined by the Court. If the trust is not supervised by the Court, a trustee may pay and receive a reasonable trustee's fee.

The guardian's fee is set by the Court based upon the value of services rendered.

All of these fees in court-supervised matters are the subject of review by the Court and, except for the fees set by the legislature, all fees in matters with or without court supervision, can be challenged in court, by or on behalf of all interested persons. (The terms executor, guardian, trustee, and attorney are discussed in detail in Chapter 7, "Your Treasures Are in Their Hands.")

**Waiving the Fee**

Many times the executor and guardian are relatives who waive their fee (in other words, they don't take it). This can be true of the trustee as well. However, when the guardian does charge a fee, it is usually very small in relation to services rendered and the trustee's annual fee may range as low as $5/10$ or $7/10$ of 1 percent of the trust assets. (See Chapter 7)

### Rumors, Rumors!

"But I've heard," confided Randy, "that if I die, the fees, costs, and taxes would eat up the estate and leave my family with nothing!" *Hearsay is often wrong.*

Janice came into my office in tears. The immediate shock and grief that followed the sudden death of her young husband had been almost more than she could take. On top of it, neighbors and friends were telling her that the costs and fees that would come from settling her husband's business and estate would leave her penniless.

After the tears stopped flowing, we began to analyze the matter. We could sell her husband's little business and probably realize about $50,000 from that. Their home was worth about $90,000 and would be clear of debt due to insurance. There was other life insurance, cash, and assets that totaled about $55,000. Altogether she would realize $195,000 after paying funeral costs and a small doctor bill.

There would be no Federal Estate Tax, due to the exemptions allowed (see Chapter 14, "The Economic Recovery Tax Act of 1981—Bugaboo? or Blessing?"), and there is no longer a State of California Inheritance Tax.

A portion of the estate had to be probated (involved in court—see Chapter 8 for explanation of probate). The balance was set aside in joint tenancy since they held their property that way, or payable by beneficiary designation (on insurance policies her husband had held). Janice served as executor and assisted in effecting a transfer of the cars, the boat, and bank accounts.

The total court costs, all fees, and other costs for clearing the $195,000 estate to Janice, including involved services in the sale of the business, did not exceed $3,000 or about 1½ percent of the total—a far cry from the $195,000 her neighbors told her it would cost.

Of course, there may be extenuating circumstances in other cases that seem similar that would cause the costs to be different. This might be true especially in other states where state taxes or additional charges apply.

Wherever you live, discuss this with your attorney. Ask him to tell you about costs and fees, and have him show you how you can save on both. It will give you the peace of mind that Janice didn't have until she talked with her counselor.

*Simply speaking, the benefits from competent professional help normally far outweigh the cost of the help.*

Before we continue on the subject of attorney's, let's take a parenthetical pause while we look at a necessary ingredient in your estate planning.

**Chapter 4**

# A Vital Need: Insurance

Let's assume, at this point, that you have started planning your estate by attending a seminar, reading books, and/or seeing an estate planning specialist.

As you continue to plan, be sure to take definite steps toward securing adequate insurance.

You do know how essential it is to have *medical* insurance, do you not? Anyone who fails to carry hospital and doctor coverage is like the fellow who drives through a heavy rainstorm on the freeway without his windshield wipers on. He's taking a terrible chance. *Fire* insurance is just as important.

### But That Isn't All

One of the best investments you can make for the future security of loved ones, and which should be part of your estate planning, is *life insurance*. The costs certainly are justified.

### Someone's Life May Depend on It

Perhaps it is because we can't quite believe that death will ever come to *us*, that we fail to realize that life insurance is vital, especially for those with families.

During the early part of this century, few people carried life insurance and the "poor farm" was a dreadful reality. Widows and dependents were often left struggling for their very existence. If they had lived in this day and age, welfare would have been offered, but their living still would not be

one of complete comfort and pride. If they'd had life in-surance, all of that would have been changed.

Let's assume your wisdom exceeds that of many, and you realize that you must provide for your family in this way. So, you may ask,

### *What kind of life insurance is best?*

Books are written on this subject, extolling the virtues of one kind of coverage as opposed to another. There are policies available such as *high initial cost whole life* and *ordinary life,* or *low initial cost level* or *decreasing term life,* and a myriad of combinations in between and on both sides.

Although all types should be explored, one definite consideration should be Whole Life Insurance. For some, this type of insurance has been a form of forced savings. A whole life policy has a cash value that increases as premiums are paid and, as time passes, this cash value can be borrowed by the insured for any purpose. Many family emergencies have been met successfully by the availability of these funds. And, of course, there is money for your loved ones should you be taken in death.

Also, take a close look at Term Insurance. This is life insurance carried for a period of time, known as "The Term" and usually for a particular purpose such as providing added funds while the children are young or going to college, to protect a business transaction, and so forth. A term policy can provide for continuation or renewal for additional terms of time and if in force at the death of the insured, it pays the policy benefits. A term policy has no cash value, you cannot borrow on it, and if it's canceled or the term expires prior to death and is not renewed, the policy pays nothing.

Then there is the Decreasing Term Insurance which provides for high benefits at the start and gradually reduces the benefits over the years, again to fit your needs, as the children are grown and become independent, and as your estate grows in other areas. The great difference between whole life insurance and term life insurance is the initial out-of-pocket costs, so your insurance, which probably should be a combination of the above, should be tailored to meet your needs and fit your budget.

All insurance is not the same cost since there is a lot of real competition in this field for your dollar. Therefore, you can find some very good buys with a little shopping.

**Please Tell Me**

Some of the most common questions asked regarding this subject include the following:

*Are the proceeds from my life insurance included in my taxable estate?*

If you retain ownership or incidents of ownership in the policy, such as the right to borrow on it, surrender it (the right to cancel it), or assign it to someone else (so they can receive the policy benefits), or the right to change the beneficiary, then, yes, the proceeds from the policy will be included in your taxable estate. This is a major reason why your insurance should be a part of your entire estate plan. There are certain exemptions from tax for insurance benefits in some states and these should be considered in your planning.

### *Should my wife have any life insurance on herself?*

Most men, probably in the interest of economy, neglect this area, to say the least. They reason that the husband is the wage earner and as such should be the one who is insured. Now that more women are moving into the labor market, that doesn't hold as true as it once did. Besides, as my wife pointed out to me, if she were to die and I had to hire some of the many things done in our home that are now being done by her, it would cost a lot of money. I now have a policy on her life. You and your wife should discuss the extent of this need and provide enough insurance to cover it.

### *Should my wife own the insurance on my life?*

The advantages gained by the practice of having the wife own the insurance on the husband's life were eliminated by the unlimited marital tax exemption contained in the Economic Recovery Tax Act of 1981. (See Chapter 14.) In the past, before the Act, this process was used by some to keep property out of the insured's estate at the insured's death, thus reducing tax at the insured's death.

Under the new law a spouse who dies can give all insurance and whatever additional property he or she has to the survivor in life or at death and have no federal estate tax on the estate of the giver or first to die. But watch out for the tax on the death of the survivor. (See Chapter 14.)

Depending on the size of your estate, your estate planner may, however, show you how to save taxes by sheltering a part of the insurance through use of a tax-savings trust—thus keeping a part of the insurance proceeds out of the survivor's estate while paying no federal estate tax on the death of the insured. (See tax-savings trust for Al and Esther, Chapter 9, and see Chapter 14.)

### What happens to life insurance proceeds if the named beneficiaries are minor children?

The proceeds are paid to a guardian for the child, who is appointed by the Court. Many problems face the guardian and children when insurance proceeds are payable to minor children. (See section on "Persons Needing the Simple Will," found in Chapter 8.)

### Who should be the beneficiary of my life insurance?

This is a question that should be asked and answered in conjunction with a comprehensive estate plan for you under your circumstances. Generally, in the small estates, everything is to go to the surviving spouse, so the insurance should likewise be payable to the surviving spouse.

If there is an estate plan that provides for a trust to care for minor children, in the event both parents are dead (see Chapter 8 for information on this subject), then the alternate beneficiary of the insurance should be the trust for the children. If the estate is medium or large and warrants estate splitting for tax savings, then the insurance benefits should be paid to conform to that estate-splitting, tax-saving plan as set forth in Chapter 9.

If you have dependent children other than those living with you, as in a divorce, you may wish to have additional coverage, with a policy payable for their benefit upon your death.

### Can I serve charity through my insurance?

Yes. This is an area overlooked by many. You can name one or more charities as alternate or as primary beneficiary. Furthermore, if you no longer need the policy proceeds in your estate for use now, you can transfer ownership of the policy to the charity or charities. If the policy has cash loan value, the charity can draw this out and use it. In this case, you not only receive a charitable gift deduction, but any additional premiums you pay are tax deductible for you now.

And, on your death, the charity receives the balance of the policy proceeds and none of it is included in your estate for tax purposes.

If your insurance man truly is knowledgeable in estate planning, he probably will introduce you to an attorney who is an expert in this field, as well, to complete any planning you do. And, if he is wise, he will hold any final decision on your part regarding life insurance until you and the attorney work out your affairs in a will and/or trusts which will work together with your insurance to serve you and yours in the best possible way.

**So What's Next?**

The next logical step in settling your affairs is to make out a will and/or a trust. But before we roll up our sleeves and dive into that, let's find out what happens when someone decides NOT to make a will or a living trust. (See Chapters 12 and 13 on "Avoiding Probate Through The Living Trust.)

**Chapter 5**

# Why Not Just Let It Happen?

Every day people die without a will, trust, or any provision for what is to be done with their property or their minor children, so the law must step in to meet the emergency.

Our laws, for the most part, are written by legislators and interpreted by judges. Most of these people are attorneys. When these attorneys leave their places in government, or in the court system, they may retire or return to the practice of law, using the very laws they wrote and interpreted to deal with your affairs.

Are laymen, then, simply pawns in a system, for the most part set up by, run for, and administered by attorneys?

Laws are just rules for people to live by. They apply to all—attorneys and laymen alike—and are most often written to try to remedy a need. When people don't obey the rules, both the rule breaker and the innocent suffer.

### Gas in Your Radiator?

Can you imagine what would happen if everyone could choose his own way to travel on the freeways? Or what would happen if anyone could land or take off at an airport without regard to instructions from the flight tower? Can you picture the problems at a busy train depot if there were no switchman? Or at a busy intersection if there were no signs or signal lights? Rules are for people to live by, and without rules we would have a great deal more difficulty living together than we do now.

So it is with the things we've accumulated—our treasures. The legislature has set up rules that apply to distribution and disposal of your treasures. These rules are designed to assist you and your loved ones. They must, however, be followed. If they are, then your disposition vehicle will run smoothly. If they're not, or if they're ignored, you're in trouble.

### Why not just let it happen?

All right. Let it happen as it will if you prefer, but be aware of this: The State has a plan all ready to go that will take care of the transfer of your things if you become incapacitated or die before you've made your own plan as with a living trust or a will.

If the deceased (the one who dies) leaves no instructions, the State *gives* the instructions, based on laws decided upon by lawmakers. These instructions from the State Legislature are known as *laws of intestacy, laws of intestate succession,* or *laws of descent and distribution.*

Sometimes these legislative directions will give a result you *would* have wanted anyway, but often that is not the case. It is not unusual for very unexpected and unfair results to occur:

> Andy died without a will, leaving a mother and sister surviving him. His wife, Bonnie, had passed away the year before. Bonnie had left five children by a former spouse. Andy's five stepchildren were all adult, had never lived with Andy, and were relatively well-to-do. They were strangers to Andy, actually. The property Andy left had been acquired during his marriage to Bonnie and by their joint efforts in a community property state. The law of intestate succession specified that all of Andy's property belonged to his stepchildren and none of it to Andy's needy mother and devoted sister.

You may agree or disagree with the result, but that is really not the point. The point is, do you want to be the one to decide where your property is to go at your death, or in the case of small children without parents, who will rear them? Or do you want that decision to be made by someone for you?

Ned's case is similar:

> Ned had come out of his divorce in pretty good shape, financially speaking. He had married again. His second wife held a good job to help pay for support of her two children from a former marriage, and the one child they had together from the present union. Except for the burden of support payments for the children from his first marriage, everything seemed to be going fine.
>
> Then the roof fell in. Ned was killed in an industrial accident at work. He had left no will. Not only that, Ned had never gotten around to changing his former wife's name as beneficiary on two of his life insurance policies, and some of the premiums on these policies had been paid from his present wife's salary.
>
> It would take pages to tell of the litigation (suing), attorneys' fees, costs, days of time lost, and sleepless nights that followed.
>
> After the litigation was over and the huge fees and costs paid, Ned's former wife, his children by his former mar-

riage, his present wife, and their son all got a part of what was left.

## But That Isn't the Worst of It

When both parents die, and they fail to give instructions or indicate their preference, the Court must find a guardian to take the children. The Court, in the absence of parents, looks to relatives. If any are available and willing, the one they choose may have been just the choice the parents would *not* have wanted. That's too bad. They can't be consulted now. At least it probably is better than the complete stranger the Court appoints in the absence of a relative after the child has been made a ward of the Juvenile Court. Or is it? Sometimes relatives tend to fight over children, appearing to want them, but once they have them, the resentments toward having to care for them begin to mount.

Besides not having the say as to where your children are to go, both the one appointed by the Court to wind up the affairs of your estate and the guardian must be bonded. (See Chapter 7, section "Keeping Them Honest.") This is an added expense your estate must bear and one you should have avoided. (See Chapter 7, "Your Treasures Are in Their Hands.")

In addition, the guardian and your child or children will have many problems to face when you are gone—problems you probably wouldn't wish on an enemy, let alone on your loved ones. (Please refer to the section on simple wills in Chapter 8, "Planning Ahead to Use Probate.") Some have cried out,

> *Can't the lawmakers change the laws of intestate succession so they will be fair?*

These laws attempt to be fair but they are, of necessity, general in nature.

> *Does the State get the property if a person dies without a will?*

Here again the laws of intestate succession go to work. If

you leave heirs who are alive to take your property and whose whereabouts are known, then they'll get the property, even if they are distant relatives. If you leave no heirs or if they can't be found, then your property will go to the State.

### Incapability or Incapacity

> *What happens if I am incapable of making a will or other provision for my property? Can it be done for me?*

If you can ask this question, you are still able to do what is necessary to put your affairs in order. Trusts are used extensively to solve this problem. (See Chapters 8, 9, 12, and 13.)

State law makes provision for the incompetent and for those who are likely to be taken advantage of by artful and designing persons if you haven't made that provision.

But don't wait until you have to have someone you wouldn't want to step in and take over your affairs. Make those arrangements while you are still able. And remember: Age is not the only event that incapacitates. Sickness and accidents also take their toll.

If, however, you are asking this question on behalf of someone you know who already is incapacitated, then you will find this next question of interest:

> *I have an aunt who is senile and can't care for herself. All the property her husband left her when he died is in her own name. Not only hasn't any planning been done, she is no longer able to do any planning. There is no will. What can be done to help her?*

First, you should proceed to have the Court appoint a guardian, conservator, or committee, to handle her affairs while she is alive. Then on her death, her property will go in accordance with the laws of intestate succession in effect in her state at her death.

## To Sum It Up

Some undesirable results of intestate succession laws are as follows:

1. Your surviving spouse and children may have to share ownership of your estate;
2. You lose the opportunity of specifying who or what will receive any of your property or specific items of your property;
3. You lose the opportunity of waiving bond for both guardian and executor;
4. You lose the opportunity of setting up a trust for care of your children;
5. You lose the opportunity of choosing a trustee and guardian who will be sympathetic to the spiritual, as well as the physical, needs of your children;
6. You lose the opportunity of planning your estate so as to minimize tax and administration expense;
7. These laws make no allowance for you to fulfill your obligations of charitable stewardship (giving to charities);
8. They include no allowance for friends.

There are many other negatives and very few positives to a course of no planning.

### Excuses, Excuses!

The doctor had just left John's hospital room. The shock was more than John felt he could bear. As he gazed out the window, he thought of Mary, his precious wife, and Mark, Ann, and Debbie, three of the finest children a man could ever want. What would his family do? How would they react to the news: Dad has three months to live?

Still, with only three months to live, John had time to make plans. He had time to put his affairs in better order and provide for his loved ones. But Tim was not so fortunate.

Tim, a happy-go-lucky insurance executive, left his office with a bounce, roared onto the freeway in his little sports car, enroute to his wife's arms and "Home Sweet Home." He loved it there. Things just couldn't be better!

Sue, his lovely daughter, was doing well in college and would be home for a visit that weekend. Jim, his handsome son, was about to be released from the service and had a fine job waiting for him.

Some lights down the freeway seemed out of place and were coming closer. Tim strained to see. Then reality registered, but too late. The lights were upon him in a blinding blast of crushing metal and shattering glass. Before he had been able to realize that the headlights were on a car driven by a drunk driver who had taken the wrong ramp, Tim was dead.

Tim's wife, Betty, had urged him many times to plan ahead and to seek professional help in putting their affairs in order. Tim had agreed to do it, but the time just never seemed right. The evenings were so short and there were so many other things to do. Spare time was for the yard, the boat, and the family.

And that planning? It's too late now.

## Not for Us!

Many times, I've heard this from young couples whose budget is tight:

> *Why should we have a will made? We believe*
> *the Lord will take care of us.*

God does take care of His own, yes, but He also has directed us to do some things for ourselves. One Bible verse says to those who have families,

> " . . . if any provide not for his own, and specially for those of his own house, he hath denied the faith, and is worse than an infidel."

Sue and Richard had five children and a very happy home. Richard was working on a scaffolding one day on a tall building in a large city. The scaffolding broke and Richard fell to his death. Sue and the children bore it bravely, their deep faith giving them strength. They continued to attend church regularly and the two children who had not professed their faith in Christ did so publicly and were baptized.

A few months later, Sue, while crossing a street, was killed, too. The children felt strongly that their mother was with their daddy in heaven, and those with whom they went to live supported that belief. Not only did the children have the legacy of their faith to support them, and a good home to go into, but because of advance planning on the part of Sue and Richard, they were left well cared for financially from provisions in their wills and life insurance.

### I Dont' Have Enough to Bother With

A pastor friend of mine was almost dragged into my office by his little wife, Jan. His first statement was, "George, I just don't have very much. To tell you the truth, the only things I have that are worthwhile are my wife and six children." As we added it up, however, Pastor Willis was surprised—as many are—at how much in the way of material possessions he did have. Although they had no insurance, and he had no retirement program except for social security, they did own a little home and a car. Before we were finished planning, we had done the following:

1.  Changed the deed on their home and the title to the car so as to avoid probate (court involvement), in the event one spouse survives.
2.  Prepared a will for both Willis and Jan, with a contingent trust to take care of those six p.k.'s (preacher's kids) in case of the death of both parents (see Chapter 8 for an explanation of contingent trusts).
3.  Funded the contingent trust with low-cost term life insurance. (The insurance is payable to the wife if living and if not living, directly to the trust, thus avoiding probate of the insurance proceeds.)
4.  Suggested the pastor have the trustees of his church consider funding a modest retirement program for him at the church's next annual business budget meeting, so as to supplement his Social Security.

Pastor Willis and Jan are delighted with the results, and the nagging thought of going on welfare or being forced to go out and find a job in case of Willis' death, while the children are still small, no longer bothers Jan.

Willis gained an additional side benefit from this experience. He learned better how to advise his parishioners concerning their financial affairs.

Beth was another who reasoned that she didn't have enough with which to bother. She had looked about her apartment, saw her used personal things, and properly reasoned that they had little value. In her thinking, all she really had of any value at all was a small savings account. She had not considered her employee death benefits, expectancies (such as gifts from relatives and friends), social security benefits, and other death benefits she had from her predeceased husband's union and lodge. There also were possible funds from a wrongful death action involving her husband's death, additional future lifetime acquisitions in the form of earnings, and her antique personal property. Her nephew, more knowledgeable in these matters, convinced her to come in to see me and we were able to work out a nice plan for disposition of what turned out to be a fair-sized estate.

## It'll All Be Gone Anyway

In the past, many have reasoned that last illness and funeral costs would likely eat up most, if not all, of what they had. This reasoning and, in the case of many, this fear, are rapidly becoming rare. With Medicare and other insurance, death and burial benefits available through employment and other sources, even the small estate is likely to be intact after a person dies and debts are all paid.

In most cases, therefore, the thought should not be, "I don't have enough to bother with," but "Do I have anyone or any organization I would like to help now or after I'm gone?" If the answer to that question is yes, then you need to make the necessary provisions during life. And as your purposes and desires are different from those of anyone else, so should the provisions you make be tailored to suit you so those purposes can be accomplished.

## What Now?

A common complaint from women has to do with husbands who won't consider a will. Like this one:

> *How do I get my husband to make a will? He won't even talk about it. He has this thing about death. We need to do something because of problems with adult stepchildren. What can I do?*

As we illustrated in Chapter 1, many organizations have people who give a short talk, show a movie or filmstrip, and answer questions relating to planning your estate and the problems and cost that can be yours if you don't plan. Use your sweet feminine ways to get him to go to one of those presentations and he may see the wisdom of getting your affairs in order.

> *Can I make a will even if my spouse doesn't care to?*

Yes, you can. We don't recommend this, just as we don't

recommend separate vacations for husband and wife. The best and most effective planning for a couple is done together. If your spouse refuses after you have pointed this out, then proceed on your own. Perhaps he or she will follow.

## Chapter 6

# *What Happens Once I Decide to Make Out A Will?*

According to *Black's Law Dictionary:*

> A WILL is the legal expression or declaration of a person's mind or wishes as to the disposition of his property, to be performed or take effect after his death.

Normally anyone who can understand what he or she is doing, and who is not a minor, *can* make a will. Some states have special provisions regarding age, marriage status, and other exceptions, so you should check your own state law in this regard.

Anyone who now owns or expects someday, prior to death, to own property or be responsible for minor children or other dependents *should* make a will.

Whether you are *single* or *married,* the need to make out a will is definite, and it should be done as soon as possible.

**It's Not All That Difficult**

Once you have decided to go ahead with a will, you should find a lawyer.

While I was speaking at a seminar in another state, this question came to me from a shy little lady:

> *The only attorneys I know frighten me or I don't understand them. Can someone else prepare my will for me?*

50

Apparently a lot of people share this feeling about attorneys, for this question has been posed to me several times. Perhaps it comes from watching TV too much, where the attorneys pictured there are either very sophisticated and debonair, or the blackest of villains associated with dark and devious deeds; or maybe personal experience has colored their thinking.

Once, while trying a case in court, I was cross-examining a witness. My intent was to get to the bottom of the matter in as businesslike way as possible. I fed the questions to her in rapid-fire succession, finally coming to, "And you *knew* he was going to take the papers, didn't you?" A hint of tears came to her eyes. She looked up at the judge pathetically and asked in a small voice, "Does he have to be so mean?"

If you have someone prepare your will for you, that is, practice law on your behalf, that person must be a licensed attorney and in compliance with the laws of your state regulating persons who practice law.

So this next question is a logical one and more important to people than many counselors recognize:

> *How can I find an attorney who is sympathetic*
> *and understanding of my feelings, beliefs, and*
> *purposes?*

Here again it is wise to find "satisfied customers" who share your beliefs and purposes. They probably can direct you to someone who will fill your needs. You can contact your favorite charity, for instance. Work with their stewardship department, and then perhaps they can recommend a counselor who won't frighten you. Attorneys are just people, with feelings, problems, and joys much like your own. If they seem a bit brusque, it is simply because they want to do the best job they can for their client in as short a time as possible. Since law is a serious business, serious-minded people often are drawn to it, and there's no doubt that some of us were behind the door when personalities were passed out. But if you insist on Mr. Charm when you search for an attorney, you might miss out altogether on Mr. Get-The-Job-Done.

**From All Directions**

Clients come to us from pastors and churches, insurance men, estate planners, other clients, business and social acquaintances, organizations, off the street, and numerous other sources. It is very important to us that the client is satisfied.

Once you decide on your man, or woman, a phone call will set up an appointment for you. Most lawyers will try to work with your schedule as best as possible. Lawyers are like anyone else, however: they would rather not take law home with them. It is better to place the call to the office, not the home, unless it is a real emergency. Some folks figure that if they can just "chat" with the counselor for a minute at home, and get all the legal advice they can in that one call, they'll cut costs. Actually, a competent lawyer is very hesitant to give any advice under such circumstances. There are too many legal pitfalls involved. The lawyer needs to have the facts concerning your case, and then apply the law to those facts before sound advice can be given.

Therefore, it is foolish for you to try to save money that way, for it normally accomplishes little and adds to your total bill. If you already are a client, the attorney charges you for time on the phone anyway, just as is done for the period you are in the office. That's because, in many cases, much of an attorney's effort is spent dealing on the telephone when handling your case, such as talking to lawyers representing the other side (as in domestic relations cases), getting research material on like cases, setting court dates, etc.

We noted in Chapter 3 that you *can* save money by coming to your first conference armed with information so your counselor's time will be lessened. So, the next question is well in order:

### *What should I bring with me to the first conference?*

When you call to set up your first conference, ask the attorney what he would like to have you bring with you. He may tell you to show up with deeds or other documents, bankbooks, names and addresses of relatives or persons who can serve in various capacities in settling your estate upon your death (see Chapter 7, "Your Treasures Are in Their Hands"), names and addresses of those you plan to name as beneficiaries in your will, etc.

Basically, you will be dealing with two categories of material possessions about which you need to make decisions:

**Real Property:** that which, generally, is something attached to ground, or ground itself. (This definition may vary in some states.)

**Personal Property;** that which is cash, stock, bonds, notes, insurance policies, employee death benefits, furniture, fixtures, vehicles, jewelry, etc.

### *How many conferences are required?*

For large complicated estates, sometimes several conferences are needed. Some of those may be with the client's accountant and other advisors. This is the unusual though, rather than the ordinary. For most, two meetings with the attorney are all that are necessary: The first one, to get all of the facts and determine your wishes, and the second, to review and sign the will. If a husband and wife are involved, they should attend both meetings together.

### *What property is a part of my estate for my will to act upon and what property is a part of my estate for tax purposes?*

- The property you hold in joint tenancy goes to the surviving joint tenant so is NOT part of your estate for your will to act on. (See Chapter 11, "Avoiding Probate Through Use of Joint Tenancy.)

- Your insurance benefits, or other property subject to beneficiary designation, go as directed in your beneficiary designation, and unless you have stated that the funds are to be paid to your estate, there is NOTHING there for your will to act on.

- Your assets in a living trust go as designated WITHOUT going into your estate for your will to act on.

- If you have only a life estate in certain property, then at your death, that property is NOT a part of your estate for your will to act on.

- The remaining property, if any, goes in accordance with the instructions contained in your will and IS acted upon by your will.

Your taxable estate will include everything subject to your will or laws of intestacy plus the insurance benefits (with certain state tax exemptions), trust assets in a revocable trust, NOTHING from the life estate, and the joint tenancy property (less the contributions of the survivor, a rule that applies only where the survivor is not a spouse). The Economic Recovery Tax Act of 1981 adopts a new and simple rule that, if property is held by a married couple as joint tenants or as tenants by the entirety, one-half of the value of the jointly owned property will be included in the estate of the one who dies first, regardless of which spouse contributed to the purchase of the property or how much. Check the Index for any unfamiliar terms mentioned in the answer to this last question.

If, of course, you have no will, the remaining property is subject to court involvement and goes in accordance with the laws of intestacy in effect in your state at the time of your death. (See Chapter 5, "Why Not Just Let It Happen?")

### *What if I've disposed of all my property in some other way before I die?*

This happens quite often, especially with husband and wife. Very often the couple will hold their property in joint tenancy (see Chapter 11, "Avoiding Probate Through Use of Joint Tenancy"), and when one predeceases (dies before) the other one, the property goes to the survivor by right of survivorship. As already stated, if all of the property is held in joint tenancy, then the will has nothing to act on and the property passes by a process called "operation of law." This sometimes happens the same way between parents and children.

A will has great flexibility and acts only where needed, but it should be a part of every estate plan whether joint tenancy, living trust, life estate, gifting, insurance, or whatever is involved. (Once again, we suggest you refer to the Index regarding unfamiliar terms mentioned here.)

## Percentages? Or Amounts?

### *In making bequests, is it important to make them in percentages instead of dollar amounts?*

Yes. If, for example, a person has a $100,000 estate at the time the will is made and wants $10,000 to go to charity and $90,000 to go to his or her children, the will should NOT read: $10,000 to charity and the balance of the estate to the children. If, due to sickness, or a depression, or for some other reason, the estate was diminished at time of death to, say, $15,000, then charity would get $10,000 and the children $5,000.

Instead, the will should read: 10 percent to charity and 90

percent or the residue to the children. Then if the estate diminished to $15,000, charity would get $1,500 and the children, $13,500. If a person wants $10,000 to go to charity and the children to have the balance, if any, no matter what the estate contained at time of death, then the first provision should be used. (Check on possible local restrictions on gifts to charity.)

### Holographic Wills and Codicils

> *I have a lot of small items, keepsakes, and personal things I want to leave to a number of persons. Can I just write a letter on this?*

I'm reminded of a clock collector who owned hundreds of clocks. Every time I walked into his house, I felt out of step. One clock near the entrance ticked in fast, staccato rhythm—tick,tick,tick,tick,tick—that reminded me of my Marine Corps days. But just about the time I had mentally increased my pace, I would move into the living room where a grandfather's clock seemed to tell me to slow down while in its

presence with at TICK—TOCK—TICK—TOCK. But the trick was keeping up with a calendar clock that had an interesting habit of hiccupping, sort of like TICK tock tick TOCK tick. Actually, it was a fascinating and fun place to visit.

The owner of these mechanical geniuses wanted each clock to go to certain people he knew, and, against my advice, put a tag on the bottom of each clock with the name of each person he wanted to remember. This did not accomplish what he wanted, nor will a letter you write, unless the letter expresses testamentary intent (shows you intended to give property away after you die) and is construed as a holographic will or codicil to your will (meaning simply a will or document changing your will). *A holographic will or codicil is a document entirely hand-dated, written, and signed in your own handwriting.* Some states do not allow holographic wills or codicils. In such a case, the will or codicil must be written, typed, or printed, and witnessed. Have your attorney instruct you as to the best way to solve this "problem" where you live.

### He Did It Right

Captain Terrance was a retired sailor. He owned a trim little boat on which he kept a number of exotic keepsakes which he had collected from around the world while serving with the United States Navy.

He had two children, to whom he wanted to give most of his things, but he also wanted a number of relatives and friends to receive an item or two.

So his witnessed will had a short paragraph giving ALL of his keepsakes to his children. Then, since a holographic codicil was permitted in his state, he wrote a codicil *revoking* that paragraph in his will, giving the keepsakes to his children, and substituted his own handwritten directions regarding keepsakes he wished to have passed on to certain individuals. He then closed by directing that all of his remaining keepsakes go to his children in equal shares. This handwritten codicil amends or changes his will and assures that his keepsakes will go to others in the way he wishes.

I have made twenty- or thirty-page wills for some who had hundreds of items to give to hundreds of people, *but* I don't recommend this procedure, for people acquire and dispose of things and acquire and lose loved ones, and so should have some flexible means of changing their property-disposing directions.

Where a holographic codicil is allowed, the attorney can show you how to do this yourself in your own handwriting. Then you can change the codicil as often as you like as you acquire additional items of property and additional persons to whom you wish to give without redoing your witnessed will.

### How often should I review my will?

As often as you have a major change of circumstances in your life. This may include a new baby, a new home, or pension benefits. Your will may have built-in provisions to take care of the new baby and many other unforeseen events, so no change is necessary.

However, as time passes, as you acquire additional assets, and as inflation increases the value of the assets you own, your circumstances may require a tax-saving will. Or, as your children become more independent and your lives more stationary and less transient, you may decide to have living trusts, or change from involved trust wills to simple wills, or vice versa. Your circumstances, rather than the passage of time, should be your motivation for review and change if needed.

### Ancillary Proceeding

*We live in one state but inherited a ranch in another from my folks. What trouble will that cause when I die?*

You should make provision for the transfer of out-of-state property to comply with the laws of that state and as a part of your estate plan. You can consider the court avoidance methods we have suggested in Chapters 10, 11, 12, and 13, such as placing your property in a trust, or deeding a life estate with the remainder to your children. But if you don't do something to avoid a court proceeding, then at your death, the property will be the subject of a separate court proceeding in the state where the property is located. This is called an *ancillary proceeding.*

*We've moved from the state where our wills were prepared. Are they valid in our new state?*

Ordinarily, a will that is valid where executed (prepared and signed) will be valid where probated (carried out by the Court). It would be wise, however, to have your will and estate planning reviewed when you take up residence in a new state, as the laws relating to how you hold title to your home and other property may vary and all of this should be coordinated with your will.

*Does the will have to be notarized?*

No, it does not.

## Witnessing a Will

### *How many witnesses do I need on my will?*

This varies according to the law of the state where you live. If a holographic will is legal in your state, then no witnesses are required. (Remember, a holographic will is a document entirely hand-dated, written, and signed in your own handwriting.) For a typewritten or printed will, most states require at least two witnesses. Some states require three, but these states recognize an out-of-state, two-witness will if that will was valid in the state where it was signed.

### *Should a beneficiary of my will sign as a witness?*

We would advise no, but there are some changes in some states in this area, so check with your attorney.

### *Who should be a witness to my will?*

Generally, any person who is permitted to testify in court can be a witness to a will. But your witnesses should be persons who have a degree of permanence in the area, are adult, and are not named in the will to take any portion of your estate.

### *Is a will made out on a printed form valid if the person signing the will refuses to have his signature witnessed for conscientious reasons and so states this in his will?*

No. This would not be a valid will. The requirements of the law concerning wills must be followed in order to protect, as much as possible, against fake and fraudulent wills.

### *Is a handwritten will legal or must it be printed or typewritten?*

All states permit all three types of wills, handwritten, printed, and typewritten, *if they are witnessed*. As we've stated before in this chapter, *some* states permit holographic wills which need *not* be witnessed. All states require witnesses (some two and some three) for the printed and typewritten wills.

### Can't my wife and I have one will we both sign?

Yes, but this procedure is inadvisable and an invitation to trouble involving questions of contract between the parties, and the necessity for both to consent to a revocation (a desire to change the will). Needless to say, when one party dies, the two can't consent, and the will may be binding on the survivor, although this is not a certainty. But why leave yourself open to these kinds of problems and questions? A husband should have his own will and the wife should have hers.

With separate wills of husband and wife, if each has provided for the other, these wills usually are called *mutual wills*.

For example, the husband leaves his property to the wife and the wife leaves her property to the husband, with the children or others taking everything on the death of the survivor of the husband and wife.

If both want the survivor to have the right to change his or her will, at the death of one, then both wills should contain a paragraph, essentially as follows: "I have not entered into either a contract to make wills or a contract not to revoke wills."

This negates the argument that, by or with their mutual wills, the couple made a contract *not* to change the wills or will at a later date. It gives the survivor the right to change his or her will in the future, a right, in our experience, most people want. If you don't want the survivor to have that right, then you should make that clear to your attorney and have him reflect your desire in your wills or in a separate written agreement.

## Liquidity

### What provisions should I make so that my wife has an immediate cash flow at my death? What

*happens to her financially during court pro-
ceedings?*

With many couples, each has a bank account in his or her
own name so cash will be available if the other dies. The
problem is that it may be necessary to probate (go through
court involvement) the bank account held by the first to die in
order to get the money in that account to the survivor. If you
want to avoid probate, your wife can have a bank account of
her own, but your name should be on it as joint tenant, as
well as hers on yours.

Many solve the problem with a Bank or Totten Trust (see
Chapter 13, "More on Avoiding Probate Through Living
Trusts"), or other simple trusts, or with a joint account, as
mentioned above, all of which can be released to the survivor
subject to local tax laws and procedures. In California joint
accounts held by spouses or anyone else are no longer frozen
and are entirely available to the surviving joint tenant.

Others assure liquidity with insurance payable to the
spouse as beneficiary. The insurance companies are very
prompt at paying claims, and your spouse should have the insurance proceeds in a few days following your death.

If the Court is involved in settling the estate, the widow or
widower can ask for an order authorizing a family allowance
which is designed to meet cash needs while the estate is going
through court proceedings.

The problem of liquidity arises most often in the estate that
is predominately made up of real estate, which often is not
readily capable of being exchanged for cash or, at least, at a
favorable price.

You should take steps now to provide the liquidity needed
so that your surviving spouse will not be in a real bind. Inven-
tory your assets, budget your liquidity needs, and then act
accordingly.

## Safely Deposited

*What should I put in a safe deposit box?*

As a general rule, you should put in the box any documents

that cannot be easily replaced if the original is lost, destroyed by fire, or stolen. Valuable jewelry, coins, and stamps are often stored for safekeeping in safe deposit boxes. Bear in mind that, in many states, the box is sealed following a death and the contents inventoried sometime after the death by a representative of the State Tax Department. Because of this and immediate need for the will and insurance policies following death, these are often stored elsewhere. If you have someone else's property in your box, that fact should be clearly stated on the property.

### Where should our wills be kept?

Your will is your private affair. Your spouse, if you have one, your attorney, and (if the size of your estate warrants it) other estate advisors, should know the details, but we don't believe it is anyone else's business.

Some want to send a copy of the will to their children or the executor or someone else who will be affected by the will. However, you may decide to have someone else serve as executor later on, and as concerned and loving as most children are, we have known more than one instance where children start looking forward to the time when they would come into money. Their attitudes and relationship to you can undergo a change that isn't always healthy. The Bible is correct when it states, " . . . the love of money is the root of all evil . . . ." so don't tempt anyone. This is your estate. Who knows? You may spend it on yourself or give it away before you die!

You can keep your will—

1. In a safe deposit box at your bank, if, according to the laws of your state, your representative or a joint user has access to the box in order to get the will at your death. In states where the box is frozen until the court has appointed someone with access rights to your safe deposit box, your will should *not* be placed there.
2. With your bank trust department, if you have named the bank to act or represent you in some capacity following your death.
3. With your attorney in his facilities provided for safekeeping.

**Forget the Rags Drawer**

Don't leave your will in your desk drawer, in a catch-all drawer, or in a little box in the closet. Too often, when one of these places is chosen, the will is lost, misplaced, or destroyed prior to your death. In some cases, it may even be destroyed *after* your death by some disgruntled person who figures he will receive something other than or more than is designated in your will, if the will somehow "disappears."

One case I had involved a substantial estate where the will was kept in a rags drawer:

> Uncle Thomas had accumulated a great deal of wealth by wise investments. He lived very simply, however, and except for splurging on a beautiful old Victorian home, he kept his money flowing into additional investments.
>
> He had insisted on keeping the original will in his own possession. When I entered the house, upon being informed of his death, I searched high and low for that will! It was nowhere.

Knowing that a young nephew of his was named in the will to receive $50,000, I felt a nagging suspicion and called him in for a meeting.

I didn't accuse him, but said, "Charles, your uncle's will has disappeared. Interestingly enough, there are only two people in the world who stand to gain by that will being gone: You and I. I would gain because it would involve litigation and thus more work for me to get the case settled. Personally speaking, I have enough work to do without having to commit a crime to get more. You would benefit, because if that will doesn't show up, some of the people your uncle left money to won't get that money because they aren't relatives. You would get it instead.

"Don't you think the District Attorney will be just a little bit suspicious when he discovers that, without the will, you would inherit $250,000 rather than $50,000 with the will? He starts a full-blown investigation tomorrow, you know. I'm sure you will be questioned at length, so I suggest you take a good hard look for that will among your things."

He got the message. That night I received a call from him. "Mr. Hardisty? I've got good news! I've found my uncle's will! I had picked up some old newspapers from uncle's house and somehow that will got in between them!"

### What if a beneficiary named in my will dies before I do?

If your will is silent as to where a gift goes if the beneficiary dies before you do and if your state law doesn't specify where it is to go in the form of an anti-lapse statute, then the gift lapses; that is, the gift fails or ceases and becomes a part of the residue of your estate. A well-drawn will does not leave this up to the law, but specifies what happens if a beneficiary predeceases you.

### Do I have to mention all of my children in my will and can I disinherit children and grandchildren?

Your should name all of your children in your will. You need not make any provision for your children or your grandchildren. You can disinherit them; but if that is your desire, it should be clearly stated in your will.

> The will of a wealthy but wise old gentleman was being read. His relatives all listened expectantly, especially his playboy nephew, Andy. No provisions had been read as yet for Andy, but finally the lawyer read, "And to my nephew, Andy Benson, whom I promised to remember . . . Hi, there, Andy!"

Now, let's talk about some important people who are going to be handling that which is dear to your heart after you are gone—your treasures.

# Chapter 7

# *Your Treasures Are in Their Hands*

As she dreamed of whom she would marry, the little girl fingered the buttons on her cape. "Rich man, poor man, beggarman, thief, doctor, lawyer, merchant, chief. Tinker, tailor, cowboy! I'm going to marry a cowboy!" She discovered as she grew up, however, that choosing a mate has little to do with a game of chance. She married a school teacher instead.

Choosing the people who will carry out the provisions of your will must not be a game of chance, either. Executor, Trustee, Guardian, Attorney, all may play an important role in your future.

Your decisions concerning these people will be vital ones. And if you *know* whom you want to serve in these capacities before you get to your lawyer's office to make out your will, time and costs can be saved. However, many couples state:

> *I'm all confused. Could you explain the difference between an executor, a trustee, a guardian, and an attorney as far as settling an estate is concerned?*

Although sometimes their duties overlap, we'll try to give a definition of each one, plus some idea of the services they perform.

## EXECUTOR

The *executor* is the person or institution named in a person's will who carries out the terms of the will. Traditionally, the word has referred to the male, and *executrix* to the female, but this distinction is rapidly disappearing.

When a person dies, the executor's job starts at once. The executor must carry on for the dead person, usually making the funeral arrangements, presenting the will to the Court, gathering the estate, continuing a business, paying bills, canceling magazine subscriptions, collecting insurance and other benefits, selling all or portions of the estate property, if necessary, completing tax reports as required, paying taxes, accounting to the Probate Court and governmental agencies, distributing what's left of the estate in accordance with the will, paying for the support of any dependents from the estate, suing, if need be, if the deceased died from an accident where another is liable, etc.

If there is no trust, and the estate is to go to minor children, the executor distributes what is left—after bills, taxes, and other costs are paid—to a *guardian*. If there is a trust to care for the estate and a guardian to care for the children, then the executor distributes to the *trustee*.

The executor's job may take a few months or longer, depending upon the problems in the estate. When the required work is completed, the executor is discharged by the Court.

The executor is *paid a fee,* but the method of determining that fee will differ from state to state, so check your local law. If you name a spouse or relative, often that person will waive his or her fee, thus reducing the amount of settlement costs.

## Who?

Generally a husband names his wife, and a wife her husband, as executor, and then they name one or more alternates. It need *not* be a spouse. It can be a relative or friend, a business associate, a bank or trust company, or an attorney. A beneficiary named in the will *may* serve as executor.

NOTE: Where there is an estate to be administered and there is no will or the deceased leaves a will but fails to name an executor, the Court appoints an administrator to do the job, with the law specifying who is entitled to be appointed.

## TRUSTEE

The *trustee* is the person or institution named by a person making the trust, or appointed by the Court, to carry out the terms of the trust.

When the executor's job is finished, the trustee's job begins, assuming a trust has been set up through a will.

The trustee takes the property and administers it as instructed by the trust instrument (the person's written instructions) and as required by law. Normally the trustee is given *wide* discretion in this administration of the estate property, as to how it is to be used for the benefit of the person's loved ones. For example, the trustee takes care of it, pays support to the guardian for the children from it, and makes decisions which the trustee considers best.

This is why your choice of trustee is *very important.* You not only want the trustee to make decisions somewhat like you would make and which would be best for your loved ones under constantly changing circumstances, but you want the trustee's philosophy of rearing children and views on life to agree with yours!

The trustee and the guardian should be able to work together for the benefit of those little ones you would rather rear yourself.

The trustee is *paid a fee* which will vary in different areas and which depends upon services rendered. A typical annual fee will be from $5/10$ to $7/10$ of 1 percent of the value of the trust assets. As with the executor, if the trustee is a relative, the fee may be waived.

## Who?

The guardian and trustee can be the same, but we recommend they *not* be because of a possible conflict of interests.

A beneficiary in the will may serve as trustee, if the beneficiary has legal capacity to receive and hold property. A minor doesn't have that capacity nor does an incompetent person. If the beneficiary is the sole beneficiary and sole trustee of a trust, the trust ceases to exist.

The choice you make should depend upon the ability of the trustee to not only serve your purposes, but do a good businesslike job of managing and working with your assets. As we mentioned before, the trustee has *wide* discretion in deciding what is best regarding your properties and your children, so your choice is of *vital importance.*

In case of death of both parents, the trustee can be a relative (parent, brother, sister, uncle, aunt, etc.), a business associate, a bank, or an organization authorized by law to serve as trustee. Attorneys often serve as trustees as well as executors.

In the case of a trust set up for children which is contingent upon the parents both dying, then a third party is named trustee. (For description of a Contingent Trust, see Chapter 8.)

With some living trusts, the one who makes the trust often serves as trustee. (See Chapters 12 and 13 regarding living trusts.)

When it comes to tax-savings trusts, the surviving spouse often serves as sole trustee even when the trust provides for invasion of principal of the trust to satisfy the needs of the surviving spouse. But special care should be taken, by the one who drafts the document, to include ascertainable standard provisions in order to satisfy the requirements of the Internal Revenue Service and assure that the assets of the tax-savings trust are not included in the estate of the surviving spouse on the death of the surviving spouse. Otherwise, the estate on the second to die may be taxed more than necessary.

In the case of tax-savings trusts for a surviving spouse where the children are adult, the trustee or co-trustee can be chosen from among the adult children. Be careful with this choice, however, as it may carry with it possible problems and conflicts. Further, if you choose an adult child as trustee, don't permit the trust principal to be used by the child for the child's own health or maintenance, or for the child's dependents, for, if you do, the income from the trust may be taxable to the trustee personally. (Refer to Chapters 9, 12, and 13 for information about tax-savings trusts.)

## GUARDIAN

The *guardian* is the person who is appointed by the Court to care for the person and/or estate of a minor child or incompetent person. One can nominate a guardian in a will, and though normally the Court will honor that nomination, the Court has the right to agree or disagree. That is, the judge can appoint a guardian who the judge feels will better serve the interests of the minor or the person who is incompetent. The Court's intervention is useful, of course, if conditions are different when you die than when you made out your will.

The guardian steps into your shoes, so to speak, so far as the responsibility for your child is concerned, except that the guardian need only look to the provision you left for the child in caring for that child. The guardian has no obligation to use personal funds.

The guardian may resign, should he or she be discontent with the arrangements, so it is very important that you set up a mechanism by contingent trust in your will or by living trust, or other means, prior to your death, to see that the guardian has sufficient funds available to care adequately for your child's needs.

The guardian is entitled to be paid a court-approved fee, but it is nominal and most people do not accept the job with the fee as motivation.

## Who?

Naturally, if only one parent has died, the surviving spouse is responsible for the child or children. In preparing for the possibility that both of you may be dead, you can name relatives or friends as guardians. We suggest you choose a couple who agree with your views on rearing children and who, if you wish, have children about the age of yours so there will be companionship. If you can find that combination among relatives, you are blessed, but if not, you should nominate friends who meet your requirements. Whatever you consider important (the arts, the out-of-doors, learning the value of a dollar, spiritual growth) should be considered when making this choice.

You will want a first choice and at least one alternate.

A bank or trust department usually *cannot* be guardian of the *person* of your child, but it can be guardian of the child's estate.

### ATTORNEY

The *attorney* (or lawyer) is a person licensed by the state to practice law and is hired to represent and assist the executor, trustee, and guardian. It is conceivable that each could hire a separate attorney, but usually one attorney represents all three.

The attorney assists the other three in completing their duties and responsibilities, both in and out of the Court.

It is possible that one person could be executor, trustee, and guardian and do everything without an attorney, but I've never known anyone who attempted this.

The attorney is paid a fee for representing the executor. The amount of the fee and the method of computing same will depend upon the laws and practices in your state. (See the section, "How Much Is It Going to Cost Me?" in Chapter 3.) The attorney's fees for representing the guardian and trustee are most often based upon the reasonable value of services rendered. As we stated in Chapter 3, all fees in court-supervised matters are subject to review by the Court and, except for fees set by the legislature, all fees in matters with or without supervision, can be challenged in court, by or on behalf of all interested persons.

### Who?

The executor hires the attorney, and that choice can be the same attorney who prepared the will (which is usually the case) or it can be someone else.

> *Should I choose guardians, a trustee, or executor who reside out of state?*

Yes, if they best serve your purposes, are willing to serve you, and there is nothing in your local law restricting your choice.

As a practical matter, though, your executor will need to

do a lot of things with your property and affairs that require the executor's presence where the property is located. Your trustee can do a much better job with the funds and property to be administered as it relates to your loved ones if distance isn't a factor.

**Keeping Them Honest**

> *Must my executor, trustee, and guardian be bonded?*

Generally, before the Court will appoint a fiduciary (executor, trustee, or guardian) of an estate, the fiduciary must be bonded to insure faithful performance of the fiduciary's duties. The bond is an indemnity bond—similar to an insurance policy which pays the estate in case there is loss caused by default or fraud by the fiduciary. If you trust your fiduciary, your will or trust should waive the bond; that is, direct that a bond is not required, thus saving your estate the cost of the bond premium.

**Chapter 8**

# *Planning Ahead to Use Probate*

## Know What You Are Doing!

You can make provision to have all or a part of your property pass to others WITH court involvement—called *probate*.

Why would anyone, in his right mind, want an estate to have to go through probate if it didn't have to? Best-selling books and articles in magazines on your newsstand decry the abuses of courts and attorneys in handling the affairs of the deceased.

"How can we avoid probate?" people ask. "Give us anything—any other course—for surely probate must be worse than even death!"

Don't you believe it. Certainly there are abuses in this field, just as there are in any field where people and money are involved, but probate is not as bad as you've heard, and in many cases is far better than anything else devised by man to solve a particular problem.

## Specifically Speaking

Probate is the legal process of proving a will, appointing an executor, and settling an estate; but by custom, it has come to be understood as *the legal process whereby a dead person's estate is administered and distributed*.

Built around it is a system of checks and balances, put there by the legislature (your duly elected representatives) to see that the estate is administered and distributed properly. In addition to the checks and balances of the law, the Court and agencies of the Court review and screen what has been done to see that it has been done properly, and in some instances have to pass on an act *before* it is done. Anyone interested in the estate has a right to seek redress from the Court, in case he believes something has not been handled correctly. Even the fees charged for the services of the executor and attorney are set by law and/or must be approved by the Court (see Chapter 7, "Your Treasures Are in Their Hands.")

Yes, where people are involved, there are bound to be abuses, but the process of probate is widely used, seldom abused, and is constantly being improved upon in areas where abuse does occur.

## SOME ADVANTAGES OF PROBATE

1. It sets rules for the *orderly passing* of property, free of lien or cloud (when others claim they have a right to your money for debts incurred by you or others);
2. It designates *who* is to wind up your affairs;
3. *It provide powers and rules* for the gathering and disposition of your assets;
4. *It provides a forum* or place where questions, claims, and disputes can be settled;
5. It provides for a special, and in most states, a shortened time within which creditors can make a claim against your estate, after which time the claim is barred;
6. It can provide *tax advantages* in certain cases, and it provides a convenient method of estate splitting for tax savings;
7. In some states, it *sets rigid limits on fees* to be charged for professional help that may be rendered. For instance, an attorney is usually needed in helping to wind up the affairs of a deceased person. That service, outside of probate, is normally charged at an hourly rate, which could result in a fee in excess of the probate fee set by law.

## SOME DISADVANTAGES OF PROBATE

1. *Publicity.* Sometimes a person who is in the public eye prefers to keep the public from knowing what is going to be

done with his or her estate, or what the estate consists of, so avoids probate for these reasons.

(Publicity is not totally a disadvantage for the average person, however, for few seem to read these published notices, and many times the publication is in a local trade paper which has limited circulation. Also, that publication satisfies the legal requirements of notice to creditors and begins a new and usually short period for creditors to make a claim against your property. After that period, creditors' claims are cut off forever.) This, in turn, allows your estate representative to proceed in a timely and orderly manner to make distribution of your property, free of cloud or threatened lien (debts by creditors).

2. *Costs* for professional help. This seems to receive the loudest complaints. (As stated before, this burden can be greatly reduced by having a relative serve your estate in a representative capacity.)

3. It can result in *delays* in winding up a person's estate if those handling the probate procrastinate, but we've found people procrastinate in or out of probate.

Let's take a look at some examples of those who have seen the wisdom of using probate in the settling of their affairs, following death.

These people generally will fall into one of three categories:

1. Persons needing only a simple will.
2. Persons needing no tax-savings trusts, but needing a will with trusts for care of children, and/or others.
3. Persons who need a will and estate-splitting, tax-savings trust.

**Keep It Simple**

As Margaret was rewriting the book, moving it out of attorney's language into layperson's language, probably the area that confused her most, initially, was the difference between wills and the variety of trusts. As we discussed it in detail, I assured her that there is an aura of confusion around these items that causes most people to shake their heads and throw up their hands, and that includes a number of attorneys who do not specialize in this field.

There are a *large* variety of trusts that can be set up and wills that can be drawn. This is where your estate-planning attorney comes in. As you lay all your affairs before him, he will be able to recommend the one or combination of several that would best serve your needs. That's his business.

But for the sake of clearing the air a bit, let's start with a summary comparison of wills and trusts, and then in the succeeding chapters, we will deal with a few of the specific types that are commonly used.

**Definition Coming Up**

As we stated in Chapter 6, according to *Black's Law Dictionary:*

> A WILL is the legal expression or declaration of a person's mind or wishes as to the disposition of his property, to be performed or take effect after his death.

But—

> A TRUST is defined as any arrangement where property is to be held and administered by a trustee for the benefit of those for whom the trust was created.

Whereas a will is used only upon the death of that person making out the will, there are trusts that can be set up by a person to be used while that person is still alive. Trusts also can be used to take care of affairs after the person has died, or a combination of both lifetime use and after death.

A will can have a trust written into it, called a *Testamentary Trust* which is set into motion by the Court after the will reaches a certain point of execution, and is used only after the death of the person whose estate it represents.

## 1. PERSONS NEEDING THE SIMPLE WILL

Some people think that simply having a will avoids probate—that when a person dies, the executor just follows the instructions contained in the will and distributes the property in accordance with those instructions. This is not what happens. *A will does not avoid probate.*

If there is property for the will to act upon, the directions contained in the will apply and the property will go as you have directed. The Court sees to it that your directions are followed.

If you have made provision to have all of your property pass to others so as to *avoid* probate, then your will has nothing to act upon. It should be filed with your local court. Nothing further is done with the will. (Avoiding probate will be discussed in Chapters 10 through 13.)

## When There Are No Minor Children

A simple will works very well in many cases where there are no minor children and no large sums to go to a person who can't be trusted with money or who needs superivsion, and where there is no need to accomplish tax savings through the will, by an estate-splitting trust.

In the simple will for the married couple, each normally provides that the survivor takes all of the property, and when both are dead, the property goes to the children. In the case where a child dies and leaves children, that share usually continues down the line to his or her children.

Charity is often served with a portion of the estate at this point, if the children are independent and it is felt they don't need funds or at least all of the funds.

## When There Are Minor Children

The simple will is sometimes chosen by people with minor children. This, we believe, is a big mistake. Should both parents die, leaving the estate to the children, a guardian is named to care for the children and estate. The estate goes into a separate guardianship account of equal amount for each child. Each account is administered and maintained by the guardian with court supervision and whatever is left when the child attains majority (eighteen in most states) is given to the child with no strings attached. An example of this is as follows:

> Jack and Angie both died in a car accident, leaving three children: Chuck, age twelve, Cheryl, age eight, and Terry,

age five. Jack and Angie left a net estate of $95,000, plus Social Security benefits.

The wills gave the property to the children, so three guardianship accounts were set up, each containing approximately $30,000.

An uncle and aunt had been named guardians, and the Court decided the children could live on the Social Security payments.

Then, Cheryl contracted tuberculosis, and a good portion of her guardianship account was used to cure the illness.

Terry proved to have a learning defect. He had to attend a special school which was costly. It was paid for, with approval of the Court, out of his guardianship account.

The guardians were very upset because every time they wanted to spend something from a child's account that had not been approved previously by the Court, they had to have the attorney prepare a petition and go with them to court to explain the request and ask for the judge's permission. This cost extra fees as well as time and the judge didn't always grant their request.

Furthermore, the guardians had to account to the Court for funds received and expended. This had to be done once a year, as ordered by the Court, which again required the services of an attorney, a court hearing, and guardian time.

Finally, the eldest, Chuck, reached eighteen. He had been able to live on his Social Security payments, up until that time, and so received his $30,000, plus interest which the amount had earned over the years. He promptly squandered the funds on such things as a flashy car, boat, gambling, and some girl friends.

When the two younger children reach majority, there won't be much left of their money, since much of it has been spent on sickness and schooling.

You can see from this case how unwise Jack and Angie were in leaving their estate outright to their minor children. You ought to hear what the guardians think of this arrangement—or maybe you shouldn't!

By the way, if there had been *no* will, the story would have been about the same, except Jack and Angie would not have been able to choose the guardians. The Court would have done that, and the choice may have been just opposite to what Jack and Angie would have wanted.

2.  PERSONS NEEDING NO TAX-SAVING TRUSTS BUT NEEDING TRUSTS FOR CARE OF MINOR CHILDREN, CHILDREN OF AGE, AND OTHER PERSONS WHO NEED A TRUSTEE'S GUIDANCE AND ASSISTANCE.

Perhaps we can best describe such a situation by looking at a case that used a *Testamentary Contingent Trust,* which, in this instance, was what we call a *Family Pot Trust.* (A Testamentary Trust is one that goes into effect after a person's death. A Testamentary Contingent Trust is set up to take care of an event that may possibly occur in the future. Every trust is set up to take care of SOME event, but we normally use the term *contingent trust* to describe the trust that provides for the *unexpected* event. A *Living Trust* also can be used to care for minor children or children of age and other persons who need a trustee's guidance and assistance. See Chapters 12 and 13.)

> Don and Pamela are young, ambitious, and on their way. They were told about the tax-saving trust, but they decided that, for now, they desire all of their property to go outright to the survivor, and when both are dead they want all of their estate to be used for their children. However, they don't want the children's lives ruined by receipt of a large sum of cash.
>
> They wish to insure, as best they can, that the children will be cared for physically, financially, and spiritually. They want them to be able to attend college should that be their desire.
>
> At a certain point in the future, when these purposes are accomplished, they want 80 percent of whatever is left to go to the children and 20 percent to go to charity (½ of that to a mission, ¼ to their church, and ¼ to a radio ministry).

## Out of a Pot (On Death of Both Parents)

The trustee takes care of the trust estate. All trust assets are held in one so-called "pot" until a certain event as specified in the trust occurs. In the meantime, the children are supported in accordance with their needs. Medical needs are paid for out of the pot, thus not penalizing one of the children for being sick. Education is paid for out of the pot, not penalizing one that might need special help.

It actually encourages a child to get a college education, for the child who goes to school has his college paid for out of the undivided interests of the other children, so a child will not have as much basis for reasoning, "If I don't go to school, I'll have that money to do anything I want when I attain a certain age."

The Pot Trust also enables the trustee to maintain one account for all of the trust assets.

The will names a guardian or guardians to take care of the children's persons if they are still minors. The trustee pays the support to the guardians as the trustee determines necessary, without having to ask for court approval or permission before or after the payment. The trustee can be an individual or an organization, such as a bank, which is authorized to serve as a trustee. (Refer to Chapter 7, "Your Treasures Are in Their Hands." for a more detailed description of the trustee's job.)

Don and Pamela hold all of their property in joint tenancy (described in Chapter 11). They have life insurance on Don's life which is payable to Pamela if living and, if not, directly to the trust, so as to avoid probate on these life insurance funds.

On the death of the first to die, there will be no probate because of the joint tenancy. Each has a will which confirms that all property, on the death of both, be held in trust and used for the support, maintenance, and education of their living children so long as any living child is under twenty-three years of age. As a child attains age twenty-three, payments to that child shall cease except for emergency medical needs. (Age twenty-three was reached by compromise of Don and Pamela. Don felt that the trust should run until the children were twenty-one, but Pamela felt twenty-five was best.) The trust authorizes the trustee to use discretion in caring for the needs of the children until they are twenty-three.

When no living child of this couple is under twenty-three, 80 percent of what is left is to be distributed to the children (with provision for a child's interest to go to the child's children, if any, if the child is not then living), and 20 percent to named charities. They hope that the children will be mature enough, at that point, to use what they receive wisely.

## I Can't Think of Anything Better

The trust seems to be the best method devised by humans to care for minor children, children of age, or persons who need guidance and assistance in the absence of those who ordinarily take care of them.

When it comes to our children, my wife and I have jokingly

remarked that we can't find guardians and trustees who we felt could do the job as ably as we, so we just aren't going to die! Of course, all parents would like to stay and have the privilege of rearing and being with their children until they are successfully launched, so to speak, but that choice is not ours to make.

**Chapter 9**

# *Continuing With Probate*

Now for the third category of people who have seen the wisdom of using probate in the settling of their affairs.

## 3. PERSONS WHO NEED ESTATE-SPLITTING, TAX-SAVING TRUSTS

One of the major concerns of an estate planner is to help you save taxes. Money saved is money earned, and I'm sure you can think of a lot of things for which you would like to see your money used, other than supporting Uncle Sam. The old uncle has his good points, though, I hasten to say. For instance, he encourages giving to charity by offering incentives for doing so. Unlimited gift and estate deductions are allowed by our Federal government for charitable gifts, which means these gifts and bequests are free of Federal tax—no matter how large. Charitable giving is a good way to save taxes, while helping others at the same time, and will be considered in our information regarding estate-splitting, tax-saving trusts.

## Pasture and Oil Wells

Perry's father and mother had lived in the old family home on 600 beautiful Oklahoma acres, with oil being pumped from one corner, for many years. Dad always wanted Perry, his only son, to have the family home when he and "Mother" were gone, with the rest of the estate to be divided equally among all four children.

Even though Perry has his own home and family close to the church he pastors, more than 1,000 miles away, Dad wanted him to move "back home" when they were gone, keep the home, and yet give the girls their 75 percent share.

Perry realized the problems that would arise from such an arrangement, the least of which would be that he would have to borrow money in order to "pay off" the girls for their share, if he didn't sell the home.

Stewardship men from Perry's church conference, with

whom he talked about it, warned him of impending difficulties if the parents didn't plan the estate properly, and finally Perry sent them to talk to his folks. But the folks wouldn't budge, and, frankly, were getting a little irritated with Perry, as were the rest of the family. In fact, at the last family gathering before Perry's dad died, when Perry brought up the subject again, one of his sisters said, "Perry, it sounds like all you're interested in is getting your hands on the folks' estate."

Perry's reply was, "I don't want *any* of their estate. I've told them many times to sell the place and spend the money on themselves. The only reason at all that I've said anything is that I don't want everything to be eaten up in taxes and costs after they're both gone; especially the taxes and costs I've been told over and over can be saved by timely planning!"

But after that, so no one would think ill of him, Perry said nothing.

Then his dad passed away. Because he wouldn't listen to Perry, much of what could have been done to save taxes can no longer be done. Everything in his mother's estate will be taxed at a very, very high rate at her death, for there will be over $100,000 in taxes that *could* have been saved. Property will have to be liquidated in order to pay those taxes, and the groundwork has been laid for problems between Perry and his sisters, due to Dad's wishes concerning the home. And this is only the tip of the iceberg.

**Parents, Note!**

Your estate may not be large. You may or may not be able to save huge sums of money. One thing you can be sure of: You can save your loved ones lots of concern before you die and much trouble after you die if you'll take the initiative yourselves to complete your planning now while you're both alive and competent.

In Perry's case, it's too late. Don't let it be too late for you and those you love.

## Split the Estate

In referring to estate-splitting tax-savings trusts, these words are intended to include the marital deduction trust, as well as the A B trust set-up. (In the A B Trust set-up, the A Trust qualifies for the marital deduction and the B Trust does not, but the amount in the B Trust can be exempt from tax by placing in the B Trust only that amount that is equal to the exemption equivalent. We'll explain this in detail on the following pages.)

The marital deduction trust is now used in both common-law states and community property states. (See Chapter 11, where we discuss common-law states and community property states and separate property.)

As a bit of background, in 1948 Congress passed a law authorizing a marital deduction. Under this law, a spouse could give a surviving spouse up to one-half of his or her adjusted gross estate free of any tax, and this could be accomplished by a Will or through a living trust, joint tenancy, insurance on the life of the decedent, and so forth.

Then Congress, by the Tax Reform Act of 1976, increased the amount of the marital deduction to one-half of the decedent's adjusted gross estate, or $250,000, whichever was greater, with certain other gift deductions. Now, by reason of the Economic Recovery Tax Act of 1981 (see Chapter 14) passed by Congress, unlimited amounts of property (other than certain terminable interests) can be transferred by one spouse to the other without federal estate or gift tax liability. (We explain adjusted gross estate and terminable interest in Chapter 14.)

But, BEWARE. This may and undoubtedly will be a trap for some, for though there will be no federal estate tax due on the death of one spouse where the property goes to the surviving spouse, there may be a huge tax on the death of the surviving spouse, which tax could be reduced or eliminated altogether with a bit of planning prior to the death of either spouse.

### Let's Split!

Estate-splitting tax-savings trusts, in this writer's experience, are usually chosen by a couple who will have an estate, including life insurance proceeds, which, after deducting amounts to be left to charity, is at least as great or greater in amount than the exemption equivalent in the year of the planning. The exemption equivalent, which is explained in detail in Chapter 14 of this book, began at $225,000 in 1982 and increases annually to $600,000 by 1987. (You will want to discuss the amount of estate that will require tax planning with your own counsel.)

Furthermore, this plan to split your estate, though motivated by a desire to reduce taxes, can also do all the things that the trust we discussed in the last chapter can do, such as care of minor children and others. (Remember Don and Pamela?)

The following case considers a testamentary plan (that is, one set up in a will to take effect only following the death of the testator—the one making the will and trust), which involves estate splitting and tax savings. (A living trust can be used to accomplish the same estate splitting and tax savings if that is your desire. See Chapters 12 and 13 on "Living Trusts.") We will not mention care of minor children in discussing this case, for we are primarily interested in tax savings.

> Al and Esther, ages sixty-eight and sixty-five, have been married for forty-four years. They have three grown children, none of whom need trustee assistance. They married the day after Al graduated from college and have had a long, happy life together. They started with nothing but a little old Ford with a rumble seat, a few wedding gifts, and some personal effects, but now they have an estate valued at more than $980,000.
>
> They saved and invested wisely, and it is their desire to see some constructive things accomplished with their assets. They told their attorney they wanted only simple wills, leaving everything to the survivor, as they trust each other to spend and dispose of the entire estate properly.
>
> The survivor would leave 90 percent to their three children and ten grandchildren, with 10 percent going to charity. When they were told they could save more than $100,000 in Federal Estate Taxes by some planning, they decided they should use tax-saving trusts.
>
> It was decided that we would draw up wills which include a testamentary trust, involving estate splitting and tax savings.

Let's compare what *would* have happened, if they had decided on simple wills, with what *will* happen, with their estate-splitting, tax-saving trusts.

## SIMPLE WILLS
### (Without Trusts)

$980,000 = Distributable estate, assuming Al's death in 1985

---

$980,000 = As Al leaves everything to Esther, the unlimited marital deduction (if there is no state tax) allows the entire estate to pass to Esther free of tax.

---

$980,000* = Esther's distributable estate on her subsequent death, before death taxes, assuming she died in 1987 or after, which will be divided as follows:
$ 98,000 . . . amount which goes to charity or 10 percent
108,940 . . . amount charged by Federal Government for taxes
774,060 . . . amount that goes to children outright

---

\* We have assumed that Esther was able to live comfortably on the income from her property, as well as Social Security and retirement benefits. In fact, if the principal was handled wisely, and inflation continued, the principal could very well be much larger than it was originally. Furthermore, we have not allowed for administration expenses or state death taxes or credits.

Let's look at this in chart form.

## SIMPLE WILLS (WITHOUT TRUSTS)

Distributable Estate, Before Death Taxes,
on Al's Death in 1985

$980,000

Estate to Esther with no tax
by reason of unlimited marital deduction
(assuming no state tax)

Esther's Distributable Estate, Before Death Taxes
on Her Death in 1987 or After
- - - - - - - - - - - - - - - - - - - - - - - - - - - - - - - -
$980,000*

| $98,000 To Charity | $108,940 Federal Estate Tax | $774,060 To Children |
|---|---|---|

\* Assumes estate stays the same. No allowances made for
administration expenses or state death taxes or credits.

- - - - - - - - - - - - - - - - - - - - - - - - - - - - - - - - - - - - - - - - - - - - - - - - - - - - - - - - - - - - - - -

### SUMMARY

$980,000 — Amount of Estate Originally

   98,000 — To Charity
108,940 — Federal Taxes
774,060 — To Children

$980,000

## WITH ESTATE-SPLITTING, TAX-SAVING TRUSTS

$980,000 = Distributable estate, before death taxes, assuming Al's death in 1985

---

$580,000 = Amount Esther receives as her community property and/or marital deduction portion

---

$400,000 = A portion of Al's estate in a tax-savings trust which will be available for Esther's use. Esther can be trustee, will receive net income for life, principal if she needs it, plus other benefits and at her death, it can go to children or to other beneficiaries without Federal Estate Tax.

There is no Federal Estate Tax on Al's death.

---

$980,000* = Total distributable estate, before death taxes, on Esther's subsequent death, assuming she dies in 1987 or after, which will be divided as follows:

$ 65,500 . . . 10 percent given directly to charity from Esther's estate

– 0 – . . . No Federal Estate Tax, as Esther's estate has a $600,000 exemption, plus her gift to charity.

400,000* . . . goes to Al's children from his trust

589,500* . . . goes to the children from Esther's estate, with no Federal Estate Tax

_____

$980,000*

---

* Once again, we are not assuming appreciation or depletion of the estate or the trust assets, and have not allowed for administration expenses on Esther's estate or state death taxes or credits on either estate.

# WITH ESTATE-SPLITTING, TAX-SAVING TRUSTS

Distributable Estate, Before Death Taxes
on Al's Death in 1985

$980,000

Estate Split

to take advantage of the exemption equivalent
with the balance being the marital deduction

$400,000*
Part of Al's Estate
in trust for Esther for life

No Federal
Taxes

$400,000
To children on
death of Esther

$580,000
Tc Esther As Community
and/or Marital Deduction

Esther's Distributable Estate,
Before Death Taxes
on Her Death in 1987 or After

$580,000

- 0 -
Federal Estate Tax

$522,000
To Children

$58,000
To Charity

* This amount can increase each year to take advantage of increasing exemption equivalent through 1987,
but never more than one-half of the community property, plus decedent's separate property.

## SUMMARY

$980,000 — Amount of Estate Originally

  58,000 — To Charity
    - 0 - — Federal Taxes
 922,000 — To Children

$980,000

So compare the two:

| Simple Wills Without Trusts | With Estate-Splitting, Tax-Saving Trusts |
|---|---|
| $980,000 — Original Estate | $980,000 — Original Estate |
| $ 98,000 — To Charity | $ 58,000*— To Charity |
| 108,940 — Federal Taxes | – 0 – — Federal Taxes** |
| 774,060 — To Children | 922,000 — To Children |
| $980,000 | $980,000 |

\*   Esther could have increased her giving to charity to equal 10% of the whole estate or whatever, but she did not have to do so to avoid taxes.

\*\*   A Federal tax savings of $108,940.

**State Taxes?**

We have not taken into consideration the State Inheritance or Death Taxes charged in all states but Nevada. This tax on either the inheritor or the estate will range from nothing to over 30 percent, depending upon the relationship, if any, of the one receiving to the one dying, and also depending upon the amount received.

This tax, if demanded by your state, should be considered as far as your estate is concerned, and provided for in your planning. Many states have passed laws doing away with direct inheritance or estate taxes, as such, but all but Nevada receive a part of the Federal Tax in an arrangement with the Federal Government, called a "pick-up tax."

We might add that there are an infinite variety of possible plans, using one or more tax-saving trusts, with varying results.

### ADVANTAGES OF THE WILL AND/OR TESTAMENTARY TRUSTS (INVOLVING PROBATE)

1. YOU determine what's to be done with your estate—not someone for you.
2. You can provide *as you see fit,* for family, friends, and charity.

3. You can *name your executor* and waive bond.
4. You can *name your guardians* and waive bond.
5. You can *provide a trust* or trusts to serve various purposes such as taking care of your spouse and/or children, insure their living and educational needs, and save taxes and estate settlement costs.
6. You can *name your trustee* and waive bond.
7. As compared with a living trust, your testamentary trust needs no implementation—that is, property *is not transferred* to it until after your death. (See Chapters 12 and 13 on "Living Trusts.")
8. You can change your will and trust any time before you die.
9. With a testamentary trust, there is *nothing for a trustee to do*—no separate accounts to keep, no dealing with trust property—*as long as you are alive.*

## DISADVANTAGES

1. You'll have to complete your plan *before you die.*
2. It will *cost* you some time and money.

**The Do-It-Yourselfer:** Occasionally, some brave soul asks,

*Can I handle things like probate myself?*

Yes, you can, although most employ an attorney to assist them. Wisconsin passed a do-it-yourself probate law. One report we received from Wisconsin went something like this:

People purchased the do-it-yourself kit, containing a packet of forms. Then, when they got bogged down, they ran to the county clerk's office for help. It finally became such a burden with the clerks "practicing law" that this had to be stopped.

Many then decided that it wasn't worth all the effort to handle it themselves and went to an attorney to do what had to be done. Others contend it has worked to the satisfaction of many.

In our opinion do-it-yourself probate really hasn't worked!

Other states have passed new and simplified probate procedures. This entire area is in a condition of flux with pressures for change. And the emphasis in state legislatures is to make it easier and less expensive to wind up a person's affairs following the person's death.

But for now, we believe the best approach is to take advantage of the many benefits available under present law—through advanced planning.

## Chapter 10

# *Planning Ahead in Order to Avoid Probate*

In most situations, there are several ways one can decide to go.

In Margaret's family, the old-timers still fondly speak of Uncle Joe Watts who lived in a cabin on Onion Creek in Oregon. Year after year, he made his home there in the mountains, working a placer mine which he had built, extracting enough gold to keep himself in food and to assure his independence and privacy.

Despite his efforts to be a hermit, however, he was not alone. He had a visitor who was attracted by one feature of the cabin that, otherwise, left a lot to be desired: a warm roof. The visitor was an eight-foot-long cougar who bedded down without fail every night to enjoy some of the comforts of home!

Not only did Uncle Joe hear the creaking as the big cat jumped from the ground to the roof, but at intervals the creature would let the entire world know he was there. (I've personally never heard a cougar scream, but when members of the family who have heard one describe it, even my hair wants to stand up on end!)

Uncle Joe was aware of the shyness of the cougar where man is concerned. He feared no sudden attack, but just to be sure the big animal didn't pounce on him unawares or out of curiosity, if nothing else, he decided to set forth a

plan of survival.

He considered several options. He could shoot the crit-
ter, but decided against it. He didn't have anything against
the cat, beyond the fact that his privacy was being invaded.
He could try to scare him away, but he didn't do that
either, because, despite the fact that Uncle Joe didn't
hanker for the company of others, it was a bit satisfying to
be appreciated by someone.

The course he decided on was simple. Since the cougar
generally left his benefactor at daybreak for a safer retreat
in the forest, Uncle Joe would merely check each morning
before he ventured outside, to be sure the feline was gone.
Peeking out the front and back doors and craning his neck
around so he could see above did the trick. When he
worked his placer mine, he would keep his "eyes peeled"
for signs of the big animal.

His plan worked fine. Winter after winter, morning
after morning, Uncle Joe Watts watched, occasionally getting a glimpse of two yellow eyes as curious as his own, and
felt no small comfort in the presence of what he had come
to think of as his "friend."

Eventually, the cougar disappeared. Uncle Joe was never attacked, and when he died, it was peacefully of old age in the cabin he had shared with another for so long.

Just as Uncle Joe Watts had to decide a course of action so he wouldn't be caught short some day, so must you if you want a plan that will work for you and enable your estate to minimize costs and avoid probate (court involvement). There are several ways you can go, some of which are as follows:

1. You can spend your money, or give it away.
2. You can invest it for life income only; or for life income plus payment to designated beneficiary(-ies) at your death; or no income to you but payment to designated beneficiary(-ies) when you die (to avoid probate the beneficiary cannot be your estate).
3. You can have only a small estate which will pass on to others by affidavit.
4. You can deed or assign your property to someone else, reserving a life estate for yourself.
5. You can place your property in joint tenancy.
6. In a community property state where the law permits it, you can enter into a community property agreement with your spouse to pass your property at your death.
7. You can enter into revocable and/or irrevocable trust agreements.

Let's consider each of these separately in these next four chapters.

### 1. YOU CAN SPEND YOUR MONEY OR GIVE IT AWAY

There are a few who choose either to spend it all or to give it all away before they die. For instance, there are Christians who have been called by God to "walk by faith," knowing that He will supply all needs. Historically an outstanding example of this is George Mueller who lived in the last century. Although there were numerous ministries in which he was engaged, he especially is remembered for his work with orphans. In being asked, "You have always found the Lord faithful to His promise, Mr. Mueller?" he is quoted in the book, *George Mueller, Man of Faith,* as saying:

"Always! He has never failed me! For nearly seventy years every need in connection with this work has been supplied. The orphans from the first until now have numbered nine thousand five hundred, but they have never wanted a meal. Hundreds of times we have commenced the day without a penny, but our Heavenly Father has sent supplies the moment they were actually required.

"In answer to prayer $7,500,000 have been sent to me. . . . No man can ever say I asked him for a penny. We have no committees, no collectors, no voting, and no endowment. All has come in answer to believing prayer."

When asked if he saved any for himself, his reply was,

"Save for myself? Never! When money is sent to me for my own use, I pass it on to God . . . . I dare not save; it would dishonor my loving, gracious, all-bountiful Father."

Amy Carmichael was one of those who followed her Savior's example by leaving riches and comfort behind and giving all to serving others for His sake, establishing the famous Dohnavur Fellowship in India. In establishing a haven for many who were searching and rescuing children—physically—from the temples of worship where they were prostituted and abused, she trusted her Heavenly Father to supply all their needs. Her faith was rewarded. He never failed her.

Nor is the forsaking of this world's goods for higher purposes limited to great saints of the past. We are personally acquainted with many who walk that path now, whose stories, undoubtedly, will not be made known in their entirety until after they have left this scene, if then.

A typical case, in our estimation is that of Dr. Bill Bright and his wife, Vonette, who left all personal desire for riches behind to heed the call of Christ to start what is now an international organization, with the goal of blanketing the world with the gospel (Campus Crusade for Christ, Inc., Arrowhead Springs, San Bernardino, CA 92414).

Another, Dr. Bob Pierce and his wife, Lorraine, started

World Vision (P. O. Box 0, Pasadena, CA 91109) to set up orphanages and help the poor, the refugee, the victims of disaster.

Dr. Clyde Narramore, a licensed psychologist, and his wife, Ruth, similarly set up the Narramore Christian Foundation so they could help people get well and reach souls with the good news about Jesus Christ (1409 N. Walnut Grove Ave., Rosemead, CA 91770).

### Giving to Loved Ones

There are some who give their property to people they love, expecting to be cared for during their remaining life. We suspect the number who choose this course are relatively few. Most elderly want to remain independent of their loved ones and *counsel to this effect is wisely given.* It's amazing how the aged can lose a lot of attraction on becoming dependent financially and physically on those around them.

Don't overlook the fact that, for those who give away their estate, there may be the problem of gift and income taxes, or should there be an attempt to keep such gifts secret, there may be penalties if such action is uncovered.

2. YOU CAN INVEST IT FOR LIFE INCOME ONLY; OR FOR LIFE INCOME PLUS PAYMENT TO DESIGNATED BENEFICIARY(-IES) AT YOUR DEATH; OR NO INCOME TO YOU BUT PAYMENT TO DESIGNATED BENEFICIARY(-IES) WHEN YOU DIE. (TO AVOID PROBATE THE BENEFICIARY CANNOT BE YOUR ESTATE.)

### An Annuity

The annuity offered by insurance companies is used by many to provide income for themselves and sometimes others in a variety of investment plans. The annuitant (the person investing funds with the insurance company) receives a contract or agreement from the company, which states that the company will pay a fixed income to the annuitant for life or a fixed period of time, with payments to start immediately or at some set future time. If the annuitant dies before the fixed period of time, any balance is paid to the annuitant's designated beneficiary. Probate or court involvement is avoided on these funds.

## Then There Is the Gift Annuity

The Gift Annuity is used by many to serve themselves and/or loved ones with a guaranteed income for life, while at the same time, investing in and serving charitable, religious, or educational works. There are several benefits to this plan:

- As a portion of the annuity is a gift, you'll receive an income tax deduction for the gift.

- A portion of the annual annuity income is exempt from Federal taxes.

- You avoid a part of the capital gain (profit from an investment) on which you have to pay taxes, on any appreciated property you may have used to purchase your annuity. Your estate is divested of this property at death since you've given it away.

- You avoid death taxes, probate, and costs on the amount involved.

- The organization will have immediate use of some of the funds you pay them for your annuity.

- Your annuity is as safe as the organization you invest with, for the total assets of the organization stand behind their agreement to make payments to you.

  CAUTION: The gift annuity is irrevocable, so once you have parted with your money pursuant to the annuity contract, you can't get it back if you need it.

We suggest you contact your insurance representative or charity. Discuss the annuity with them and your attorney to decide for yourself if this is an estate-planning tool that can serve you and yours.

## Life Insurance

All proceeds paid for life insurance will not be in your estate and you avoid probate on these proceeds—plus the funds payable under the terms of the insurance contract at your death, unless the funds are payable to your estate.

## Pension, Retirement, and Similar Plans

In recent years, rapidly increasing interest is being shown in the use of pension and retirement plans. People have seen the need to provide for retirement years and also reduce taxes by use of a tax shelter before they reach retirement. Employers and unions have bargained over this issue for years and have come up with a variety of plans that are serving many today. However, little was being done for the individual who was not a part of a big company. The HR-10 (also called Keogh) retirement plans for the self-employed have been in use since 1963 and have now been substantially liberalized by provisions contained in the Economic Recovery Tax Act of 1981 and in the Tax Equity and Fiscal Responsibility Act of 1982. In 1974 Congress saw the need to regulate and protect against abuses in the whole area of retirement, so passed the Employment Retirement Income Security Act of 1974, referred to as ERISA. Along with regulations, the act permits individual retirement accounts (referred to as IRA's) for approximately 40 million Americans not covered by any other qualified retirement plan.

The Economic Recovery Tax Act of 1981 also makes changes in the rules regulating IRA's (Individual Retirement Accounts). IRA accounts are set up with local banks, savings and loan associations, and others. Any self-employed individual, less than 70½ years of age, can place in this account annually, the smaller of $2,000.00 or 100% of the individual's income, and this sum is a deduction on the individual's income tax return. The individual *can* withdraw from the account any time between the ages of 59½ to 70½, but *must* start to withdraw from the account on reaching age 70½. If the individual has a non-employed spouse and a spousal IRA is established, the individual can place up to $2,250.00 instead of $2,000 in an IRA annually. If both spouses in a marriage are employed, each can set up a separate IRA account and place up to $2,000.00 each in the accounts annually, all of which is an income tax deduction.

Pension and retirement plans are many and varied, as are

HR-10 (or Keogh) and IRA plans, but here again the plans can provide for you and/or your loved ones and bring you tax savings. Furthermore, you avoid probate on all funds used to purchase your plan and all death benefits payable under the terms of the plan to beneficiary(-ies) other than your estate.

## United States Savings Bonds

United States Savings Bonds are pretty much in a class by themselves. They may be registered so as to pass to a named beneficiary on the death of the owner. For instance, the registration might be: John Smith, payable on death or P.O.D. to Janice Toms. The funds from the bonds pass to the beneficiary free of probate.

You may want to check with your attorney to determine if this procedure is permitted in your area with any other type of securities.

3. YOU CAN HAVE ONLY A SMALL ESTATE WHICH WILL PASS ON TO OTHERS BY AFFIDAVIT.
This will depend on the laws of your state. In California, if there is no real property, and the estate does not exceed $30,000, plus certain other described property, the estate can pass by affidavit without court involvement in what is called a summary proceeding. Other states have made similar provisions for this affidavit or summary proceeding with legislatures acting to increase the size of estates that are included.

The law permits certain persons to obtain the property after your death by simply supplying an affidavit in compliance with the law to the one holding the property. Check you local state law in this regard.

4. YOU CAN DEED OR ASSIGN YOUR PROPERTY TO SOMEONE ELSE, RESERVING A LIFE ESTATE FOR YOURSELF.
Most often this is done by the elderly, deeding or assigning property to their children who will receive their property on their death anyhow. Here again, gift and possible income taxes must be considered. Also, keep in mind that the moment of death is an unknown, and there may be a tomorrow

under different circumstances. You may *need* your property yourself before you die.

There are some who have used the so-called *cross deeds* which meant deeding property to each other, to children, and other persons. These deeds were then placed in a safe or other place for safekeeping. Then, at the death of one of the persons involved, one of the deeds, the appropriate one, would be taken from its storage place and hurriedly recorded.

For example:

> Mom and Pop had a daughter, Mary, who was twenty-two years of age. They lived in a place Pop's folks had homesteaded some years before. They saw no reason why the survivor should have to go through a lot of red tape, or possibly pay taxes on the property if one or more of them died.
>
> So Pop deeded the property to Mom, and Mom deeded the property to Pop, and both deeded the property to Mary. They put the three deeds in an appropriate storage place.
>
> When Pop died, Mom simply took out the deed that said the property was hers and presented it to the authorities, who recorded it.

This effort to make a testamentary disposition by deed, is *not* valid (a testamentary disposition, remember, is a giving of property, which gift is not to take effect until the giver dies). It is an attempt to bypass procedures that make it safe for you or me to buy property with assurance that there are no government liens (demands that debts be paid) for taxes, or other possible liens against that property. A title company, or other insurer of title, won't insure the title to a property so you can sell it, until the record shows the title has been properly cleared of liens and transferred, as through probate, joint tenancy termination, or other proper legal procedures.

If the death of one who signed the deed is not known by the insurer, then the insurance won't cover claims that may arise from failure to properly pass title on death, and all who are involved with the property are faced with possible future trouble.

# Chapter 11

# *Avoiding Probate Through Use of Joint Tenancy*

Thus far we have discussed four ways by which one can avoid probate. THE FIFTH WAY IS BY PLACING YOUR PROPERTY IN JOINT TENANCY.

Any two or more persons, related or not, may hold property in joint tenancy and the property passes to the survivor or survivors on the death of one. This passing is not automatic, as some think, and procedure for passing will depend on local law. But, this form of ownership does have the advantage of allowing the property to pass to the survivor without delays of probate and court administration costs.

Though many studies have been made and published on the pitfalls of joint tenancy, it is still one of the most widely used methods of property ownership. Probably this is because people have seen it used by others to effect a relatively simple and painless transfer of property on the death of one of the joint tenants to the other(s).

Over the years, many have come to us, on the death of one of the joint property holders, for assistance in clearing the title, and frankly, most of them have been pleased with the results.

Since there *are* pitfalls and possible problems with joint tenancy, let us consider some of the basics so that you can decide if this is the route you wish to follow.

A. *All documents creating joint tenancy must make it clear that this is what you intended, so should contain the words, JOINT TENANTS or JOINT TENANCY.*

> Ed, a knowledgeable businessman, wanted everything he owned to go to his wife. He wanted to avoid probate and chose the joint tenancy route to accomplish this. When asked by his estate planner to show the deed, Ed said, "Don't worry. It's in joint tenancy."
>
> Ed suddenly died several weeks later, and his wife and the estate planner found that the deed read in their names as "husband and wife." This was not a joint tenancy, but tenancy in common (each owning one-half). The necessary words "joint tenancy" or "joint tenants" were not on the deed. It was necessary to have Ed's one-half of that very expensive home go through probate to get it to the wife. Needless to say, Ed's wife was very unhappy. (We have a simplified community property, set-aside proceeding available now in California for a case like this, but it wasn't available then.)

Your deed and other evidences of title should be shown to your estate planner so that your estate plan will function as intended and for your benefit.

A couple shared:

> *Our property reads, "William Birdy and Anita Birdy." Is that joint tenancy? Or should we have put the word "or" in place of the "and"?*

Your property will not be joint tenancy until the words "joint tenants" or "joint tenancy" are on the documents. Substituting the word "or" instead of "and" will not change the situation.

> *How about cash? If we have "and" and "or" between the names on our bankbook, does that make it joint tenancy?*

No. The signature card you signed at the bank rules, and this card will specifically state how the account is held. If a husband and wife are involved and you don't specify to the contrary, more often than not, the bank assistant setting up your account will have you sign a joint tenancy signature card.

B. *A tax may be involved.* As a general rule the entire value of the joint property is included in the gross estate of the first to die *except* that part the survivor can prove was contributed by the survivor. *Accurate records should be kept* showing how the property was acquired—that is, by purchase, gift, inheritance, and so forth. These records of proof are often not available. Under this general rule the rest of the joint property is taxed, for it is considered a gift to the survivor.

The Economic Recovery Tax Act of 1981 (see Chapter 14) provides a new special rule for certain jointly owned property of a husband and wife. The Act provides that where property is held jointly by spouses, with right of survivorship, when one spouse dies, one-half of the value of the property is included in the estate of the first spouse to die regardless of who contributed to the purchase of the property or the amount of the contribution.

### Is it wise then, to hold our home in joint tenancy?

If there are no overriding adverse tax or personal estate-planning problems, this is an expedient way to hold property.

- If use of joint tenancy will add tax burdens to the second to die or defeat your plan to split your estate by use of a trust, and thus increase Federal Estate and State Inheritance Taxes,

- If use of joint tenancy will deprive you of maximum stepped-up basis and result in added capital gain tax on sale of property,

- If use of joint tenancy will result in additional tax due to the property being included in both of the tenants' estates,

- If there are other problems your own counselor points out

which outweigh the advantages—

then you should *not* hold your home in joint tenancy.

In California, many attorneys solve the problem of property ownership with the use of a *Community Property Agreement* (community property is discussed later on in this chapter) in conjunction with an estate-splitting, tax-saving trust (Chapter 9, "Continuing With Probate"). This agreement normally is used only in estates where there are tax considerations. A husband and wife will agree that their property held in joint tenancy is community property. Then, at the death of one, the agreement rules and is used to avoid the adverse tax consequences of joint tenancy.

One of the major problems that can come from passing property by joint tenancy is the problem of capital gains tax on sale of property by the surviving joint tenant.

For example, Tom and Edna Peck owned a house purchased in 1948 for $30,000 that was worth $190,000 when Tom died on February 10, 1982. Under the new law only one-half of the value of the house is included in his gross estate. Nonetheless, Edna has a joint tenancy termination, and the property was placed in her name. Then in November, 1982, she sold the property for $215,000 and moved into a rented condominium.

Under the new law her tax basis is the $95,000 (the $95,000 being one-half of the value of the house included in Tom's estate), plus $15,000 (half the original cost), or a total of $110,000, resulting in a $105,000 capital gain.

Fortunately Edna can elect to completely exclude the gain realized on the sale of her personal residence. Under the Economic Recovery Tax Act of 1981 the $100,000 exclusion provision of the Revenue Act of 1978 was increased to $125,000. This is a provision that allows the once-in-a-lifetime exclusion of up to $125,000 capital gain for taxpayers who are fifty-five years or older before the sale and who have used the property as a personal residence for three years out of the five-year period immediately preceding the sale.

C. *Once a joint tenancy is created, the property may be affected by the lives and problems of all tenants.* One widow asked:

> *My husband has died, so should I place my property in joint tenancy with my two adult children, so as to avoid probate?*

Many older persons do just that. They want their property to go to their children at their death, anyway, so feel they may as well get a jump on it with joint tenancy and avoid probate.

Most people trust their loved ones, and in many cases, such an arrangement works to the mutual good of all concerned.

### But There Are Risks Involved

> On a hunting safari, the wife yelled, "Bill! Come quickly! A wild tiger has just gone into mother's tent!"
>
> The husband continued to sip a cool lemonade as he answered, "Well, he got himself into that mess; let him get out of it!"

Some people get into some real messes, not because they intend to, but because they act in ignorance of the law. And sometimes they can't "get out of it" at all!

When a joint tenancy is set up, it is a completed transfer and subjects the property to claim from the creditors of all the joint tenants.

> Grandmother Daren had two grandsons to whom she wished to leave her property, a small farm. She decided to place the farm in joint tenancy to make it easier for the grandchildren at her death, and because she thought it might help the younger, Darryl, settle down and take some responsibility.
>
> It seemed to help the boy for awhile, but he soon grew restless, left to bum around the country a bit, and in the process, piled up some debts.
>
> Meanwhile, Perry, the older grandson, suffered financial losses which occurred when his baby daughter was born with complications.

Although Perry seemed to be making progress in getting his huge medical bills paid off, Darryl continued to pile up debts.

Then the time came when Grandmother decided she would be better off in an expensive rest home, where all her needs would be cared for. That necessitated selling the farm. Preparations were made, but just then, Darryl's creditors decided to sue, and they won a judgment. The proceeds from the sale of the farm went to pay his debts. Now Grandmother Daren had no farm nor had she enough money to keep her for any length of time in the rest home.

You see, the judgment against Darryl became a lien against the property, and it was easier to pay Darryl's debt out of the sale proceeds than try to prove in court that the property really belonged to Grandma and the joint tenancy was only a convenient arrangement between relatives.

Suffice it to say that the decision to place your property in joint tenancy with your children should be made only after careful consideration of the advantages and disadvantages of this move.

In some states, a joint tenancy between a husband and wife involving real estate is known as *tenancy by the entirety.* Neither spouse has a right alone to terminate that joint tenancy.

### *Does joint tenancy property automatically pass to the surviving joint tenant?*

Title passes to the surviving joint tenant at the instant of death of the first to die so that no property interest is in the estate of the first to die for probate purposes. There *are requirements* that must be met so the survivor can have CLEAR title. Requirements will vary depending upon the state that has jurisdiction over the property at the death of the joint tenant.

### *What procedures take place regarding joint tenancy property when one of the joint tenants dies?*

I'll cite a typical case in our experience: Mrs. Terrance was left with the following when her husband died: a modest home full of furniture, two cars, two bank accounts, some stock, a Social Security death benefit, and a small life insurance policy.

Her assets had a total value of approximately $95,000. All of the property that had title was registered in joint tenancy. The furniture had no registered title, and the insurance contract named Mrs. Terrance as beneficiary.

- We completed a short affidavit to be signed by Mrs. Terrance as the surviving joint tenant.
- We recorded a certified copy of the death certificate and the affidavit in the recorder's office where the home was located.
- Mrs. Terrance then took the title papers on the cars to the Motor Vehicle Department and they assisted her in completing a simple affidavit, effecting the transfer of the autos to her.

- An insurance agent friend was happy to assist her in collecting the insurance benefits.

- She took her stock consents to her broker and he effected transfer of the stock to her.

- The funeral home assisted her concerning the Social Security death benefit.

- That left only the furniture, which passed to her as community property.

It is possible that trouble can come where, in the absence of a will, the furniture might not be community property and would go part to the widow and part to the children. But secondhand furniture is not usually worth a lot, so few care, and generally the family desires that the widow have all of it, anyhow.

In Mrs. Terrance's case, there was no federal or state tax to pay, no basis problems, no court costs, and only a relatively small attorney's fee. (There may be a state tax where you live on this size estate, but there will be no federal estate tax.)

Actually, Mrs. Terrance could have completed all of the above transactions herself. There is no law that requires anyone to hire a lawyer in such a case. The representatives of the State Inheritance or Death Tax Office are usually willing to assist.

However, Mrs. Terrance chose to use a lawyer, simply because it was much easier for her that way, and she had no fears about having done it right.

Typical questions asked me in seminars are:

### *What property can I hold in joint tenancy?*

Some property cannot be held in joint tenancy because of a prohibition to that effect. For example, a pension agreement may prohibit such a holding. Where no such prohibition exists, then any property can be held in joint tenancy. But, of course, the creation of a joint tenancy requires a written declaration to that effect.

*If a couple have property in joint tenancy and
have minor children, and they have reciprocal
wills leaving their property to each other and
then their children, and the whole family dies
in a common tragedy, who receives the estate?*

One-half will go to the heirs at law, of the husband, and
one-half to the heirs at law, of the wife, both in accordance
with the laws of succession in effect in the state of residence
of the couple at the time of their death.

In a case where just the husband and wife die at the same
time, the law speaks directly to this. The Uniform
Simultaneous Death Act is in effect in most states, and where
it is, and the deaths occur at the same time, or in a situation
where there is not sufficient evidence that one survived the
other, then the property of each passes as if that person *had*
survived the other. In this modern day when so many are
together as they travel, this is a real concern.

The joint tenancy holding of husband and wife seems fair
and simple. But where one spouse, for example, holds a large
separate estate and the other spouse a small estate, and there
is a desire to obtain the tax-saving benefits of the marital
deduction, by equalizing the estates of the husband and wife
on death, then the will of the spouse holding the large estate
should contain a paragraph overcoming the effect of the
Uniform Simultaneous Death Act. That paragaraph would
say that the spouse with the large estate died first, so a part of
that estate could pass to the survivor to equalize their estates
for taxation. Discuss this with your attorney.

*If we hold our property in joint tenancy do we
both need wills?*

If you could be sure that one of two joint tenants would die
first, and that the survivor would be mentally, physically, and
emotionally capable of making a will, then the answer is no,
you don't need two wills. The problem, though, is evident.
You don't *know* which one will die first, or if both will die
simultaneously. If one joint tenant dies first, the survivor

may be injured and unable to make a will. Therefore, it is recommended that each joint tenant have a separate will.

### What property is subject to my will if I hold all my property in joint tenancy?

Rarely does a person hold *all* of his or her property in joint tenancy. If we assume all is held in joint tenancy, then at your death, if your joint tenant survives you, all of the property goes to that surviving joint tenant and there's nothing for your will to act on. If your joint tenant dies before you do, then the property belongs to you and is subject to your will. If you and your joint tenant die at the same time, one-half of the property is subject to your will. This is why we always recommend a will, even when people hold everything in joint tenancy.

### Do death taxes have to be paid on property held in joint tenancy?

Yes, death taxes must be paid on property held in joint tenancy subject to a deduction for provable contributions to the purchase of the property by the survivor, a deduction for indebtedness on the property, and subject to a special rule under the Economic Recovery Tax Act of 1981 for jointly owned property of a husband and wife, as previously explained in this chapter.

**Check It Out**

Before deciding to make joint tenancy a part or all of your estate planning, you should discuss some of the pros and cons of this form of ownership, as they apply to your own property, with your attorney. Then decide what is best for you and yours.

### ADVANTAGES OF JOINT TENANCY

1. *It can be used to avoid probate.* On the death of a joint tenant all the deceased owned in joint tenancy belongs to the surviving tenant or tenants without court involvement.

2. *The ownership interests are equal.*

3. It is a *convenient method* of holding property and one which is familiar to people.

4. *It is an estate-planning tool.* If the estate has no tax problems and won't create some for the estate it goes to, then joint tenancy can be very effective and a useful tool, if used in conjunction with a will and your complete estate plan.

## DISADVANTAGES OF JOINT TENANCY

1. There is a possibility of *double taxation, heavy tax burdens, and capital gain problems* on subsequent sale for the survivor.

2. The property goes to the surviving joint tenant (where the joint tenancy consists of two persons) and *is not subject to the will* of the first to die.

3. There may be unexpected *gift tax consequences.*

4. Neither party in the kind of joint tenancy (between spouses), known as a *tenancy by the entirety,* has a right alone to terminate the tenancy or transfer his or her own interest. (Not all states recognize tenancy by the entirety.)

5. If the joint tenancy is relied upon as a will substitute, and the tenants die in a *common disaster,* many resulting problems may occur.

6. The parties and property in a joint tenancy arrangement can be *subject to creditors' suits,* should one of the tenants incur debts.

7. *Personal estate-planning desires* such as a desire to serve charity, or the need to provide for responsibilities in a second marriage, and so on, *may not be met.*

### Another Way—Community Property

A SIXTH WAY TO AVOID PROBATE IS BY ENTERING INTO A COMMUNITY PROPERTY AGREEMENT WITH YOUR SPOUSE TO PASS YOUR PROPERTY AT YOUR DEATH—IF YOU ARE IN A COMMUNITY PROPERTY STATE WHERE THE LAW PERMITS IT.

To dispel any confusion, let's ask,

*What's the difference between community*

### property, joint tenancy property, and separate property?

In California, *community property* is all property acquired by the joint efforts of a husband and wife during marriage and before separation (which we hope will not take place) and which is not separate property. Community property is owned by a married couple in a kind of marriage partnership, each partner owning an undivided one-half. (If you live in a community property state, check the effect of a separation on property acquired after separation in your state.)

*Joint tenancy property* is property owned by two or more persons in equal shares by a title created by a single instrument (something in writing), expressly declaring the title to be a joint tenancy. Joint tenants can be, but need not be, related by marriage or otherwise.

*Separate property* is that property acquired by an individual before marriage or after marriage is terminated. During marriage, a person can acquire separate property by inheritance or gift. Some other property acquisitions during marriage will be separate property, but this depends upon the law where the person lives. Regardless of when acquired, separate property *remains* separate property until it is changed by the owner to some other form. This change, however, may be unintentional. For example, in California, separate property can be commingled (that is, mixed) with community property so that it can't be traced, in which event it becomes community property. You cannot unintentionally change separate property to joint tenancy property, however, as joint tenancy requires a document in writing to that effect.

### Can community property be held in joint tenancy for convenience?

Yes, so long as the parties agree that the property is to remain community property, then it can be held for convenience in both names, as joint tenants, or in some other form of property holding.

### What is a community property state and what

*is a common-law state?*

Eight of the fifty states are community property states: Arizona, California, Idaho, Louisiana, Nevada, New Mexico, Texas, and Washington. Puerto Rico also has community property. All of the other forty-two states are common-law states. Joint tenancy exists in all of the states, but community property in only the eight.

In the eight community property states, a husband and wife each own an undivided one-half of the whole, including earnings and savings therefrom.

When one spouse dies, the survivor continues to own his or her one-half, and the other half is subject to disposition by the will of the dead spouse.

At one time, in the forty-two common-law states, a widow had a right to a portion of her husband's estate, called "dower" and a widower had a right to a portion of his wife's estate, called "curtesy." Most common-law states have abolished dower and curtesy and others have modified it. The modern approach is to give widows and widowers an identical fixed share of the estate of the other. You should check your own state laws in this regard.

**Helpful Laws**

Some states have passed various laws that facilitate the transfer of estates. For example, Washington (a community property state) has a law that authorizes a *community property agreement* between spouses which is a contract that takes precedence over a will on the death of the first spouse to die and effects a transfer of the community property to the surviving spouse without probate. But watch out as this community property agreement can be used to convert separate property to community property, and it also can be used to balloon the estate of the surviving spouse (with resulting death tax burdens similar to what happens with joint tenancy.)

It is used by many, however, because of the ease of transfer on the death of a spouse, but is generally recommended only where there are no tax problems, with estates in the $100,000 range, and then only with advice of an attorney in conjunction with a will and estate plan, just as we recommend with joint tenancy.

Wherever you live, whether in a community property or common-law state, your own counsel can advise you of the latest procedures available to you and designed to simplify the process of estate transfer.

But now, on to further ways to avoid probate!

## Chapter 12

# *Avoiding Probate Through the Living Trust*

THERE IS A SEVENTH WAY TO AVOID PROBATE: THROUGH THE **INTER VIVOS** OR **LIVING TRUST**.

A TRUST is defined as any arrangement where property is to be held and administered by a trustee for the benefit of those for whom the trust was created.

A LIVING TRUST is a trust that is set up to operate during the life of the one setting up the trust.

### Two For Your Money

There are living trusts which are *revocable* and living trusts which are *irrevocable*.

If the living trust is *revocable,* you can revoke it, or in other words, change your mind and have some or all of the trust property returned to you during your life. As a living trust, it can operate while you are alive and after your death.

If the living trust is *irrevocable,* it cannot be revoked. That is, you cannot change your mind and take your trust property back while it is irrevocable. No one else can revoke this trust either, except on proof of one or more of the following:

- That there was fraud, deception, incompetence, or the like involved in the making of the agreement;

- That the terms of the agreement are unlawful or impossible to complete;

- That the sole trustee is the sole beneficiary (i.e., the same person)—resulting in a merger of interests; or

- That all the beneficiaries (none being a minor) agree on a termination, and the Court is satisfied that the purposes of the trust have been accomplished.

Since both types of these living trusts have advantages and disadvantages, let us consider them separately.

## USE OF THE REVOCABLE LIVING TRUST IN AVOIDING PROBATE

### Out of His Mind

Martha, an elderly widow, had been my client for years. She had a will to take care of her substantial estate when she died. I suggested she replace her will with a living trust. Martha agreed, as she wanted to avoid probate of her estate and save fees and costs. I prepared a living trust and sent it to her to review before our meeting.

When we met for the signing, Martha's daughter came with her and began the conversation by saying, "Mr. Hardisty, my mother and I took these papers to our accountant in the city and he said, 'Your attorney must be out of his mind.' "

I said, "Why would you think he'd say a thing like that?"

She answered, "He read over the papers. Then he just sat there shaking his head. He said, 'This attorney is doing himself out of an almost sure $50,000 fee when you die, Martha. He must be out of his mind.' "

So we happily proceeded. Martha gladly signed her trust, and I finished the day satisfied I'd done something worthwhile for my client.

## FOR ALMOST EVERYONE

### The Not-So-Wealthy Widow

The revocable living trust is used extensively by not-so-rich widows as well, to save costs, fees, and court involvement. It is especially useful where she and her husband had a simple will or had done no planning prior to his death and the estate comes to her by reason of the will or by joint tenancy survivorship, beneficiary designation (as with insurance and pension funds), or community property set-aside.

Evelyn is a case in point:

> Her husband, Jim, died. Their three children were all adults and married. After clearing the property so that she owns it outright, she has roughly $150,000, consisting of—

| A home (clear of debt) | $90,000 |
| Stocks and bonds | 15,000 |
| A car, furniture, and personal property | 15,000 |
| Cash from savings and Jim's insurance | 30,000 |

In addition, she has Social Security and a small pension from Jim's former employer. With stock dividends and interest on the bonds and savings, Evelyn could live very comfortably and travel to faraway places occasionally.

At her death she wants roughly 80% of her estate to go to her children and grandchildren and 20% to go to her favorite charities. In addition to a revocable living trust for most of her property, she placed $30,000 in *three simple revocable living trusts,* one each with three of her favorite charities. The trusts provide that she will receive a stated payment quarterly and that if she needs all or part of the funds, she can have them on request.

Whatever remains in the trusts, if anything, at the time of her death, will belong to the named charities. This removes the funds in the trusts from court involvement and taxes and makes them immediately available on her death to the charities.

The balance of her estate is well within the federal estate tax exemption so that no federal estate taxes will be payable at her death, and her children will receive the balance of her estate without probate delay and costs, and with no state inheritance tax for this California estate.

## The Discerning Couple

Ed and Marcy have an estate of $700,000 and have estate-splitting tax-savings testamentary trusts set up in their wills.

When either of them dies, the survivor will have to be involved with probate. The survivor, as executor, probably will waive the executor's fee, but the statutory fee set by the legislature in California for the attorney, on half of this estate which would be probated, is $8,150, plus court costs, newspaper publication costs, and so on. In addition, the survivor will have a lot of work to do as executor and will have the publicity of probate plus months, and sometimes years, of delay in settling the estate.

Then, when the survivor dies, the whole probate proceeding is repeated. Whatever estate belongs to the survivor will go through the mill again. For example, if the survivor's estate is valued at $500,000 at the survivor's death, the fee for the executor will be $11,150 and the fee for the attorney will be $11,150, plus court and other costs, delay, and publicity.

When it was pointed out to Ed and Marcy that, should they choose to use a revocable living trust: as much as 90% + of the fees, costs, and delay can be avoided; while they are both alive, no fiduciary tax returns will be required of them as they administer the trust; there will be no probate for the survivor when the other dies; and there will be no probate for the family when the survivor dies, they decided to have a revocable living trust to serve them in their planning.

## The Younger Couple

*My husband and I have an estate of a little over $160,000. We're in our forties with two minor and two adult children. Should we have a living trust at this time?*

I would advise you to weigh this decision very carefully. You are still young enough so that there is a strong possibility that you will acquire, dispose of, move, change relationships, change banks, get new friends, and so on. Tying yourselves to a living trust at this time may create undue burdens, since your estate can pass to the survivor at the death of one of you without probate. After that, the survivor can have a living trust in order to avoid probate for the survivor's heirs. Of course, you are taking the chance that the survivor, due to age, injury, or sickness, will not be able to be involved in the decisions which would need to be made at that later time in order to have a living trust.

A living trust costs more initially to prepare than a will with a contingent trust, which you need for your children and grandchildren. If you can look at this planning somewhat the way couples look at their life insurance, and are willing to pay a little more now and don't mind the small amount of management that is involved with a living trust, then the living trust may be for you even at this stage in your lives. With it, you can accomplish the same things for your children and grandchildren. In addition, you will have the other advantages the living trust offers.

**Thanks To Washington**

Thanks to the present administration in Washington, the rules and regulations (such as those no longer requiring fiduciary tax returns for revocable grantor trusts) make living trusts a lot easier to maintain over a long period of time. The living trust is now being used by a rapidly increasing number of people to avoid probate, save legal fees, court costs, executor's fees, time, and trouble, whether they are single or married, young or old, and regardless of whether they have a lot or a little of this world's material goods.

**Be Careful!**

Where your trust is revocable, your trust property won't be included in probate, but it will be included in your estate for tax purposes as though the trust did not exist, this being one of the differences between a revocable and irrevocable trust. (See next chapter.)

Before you use the revocable living trust to serve you and

yours in estate planning, you should check with your attorney as to its tax effect and use in your state.

## ADVANTAGES OF THE REVOCABLE LIVING TRUST

1. You *see* your trust *work*.

2. If you are not your own trustee, you *observe* your *trustee* in action.

3. You *avoid probate* and the trust can be used to *avoid ancillary probate*—that is probate of property in another state.

4. You *avoid* the attendant *publicity* of probate.

5. You will probably *save* your estate a substantial amount of *fees* and *costs*.

6. You can provide for *uninterrupted management* in case of incapacity.

7. You *avoid interruption* of *management* at death.

8. It's a good way to pass property to *charity,* and *save taxes* at death.

9. You can *change your mind*.

## DISADVANTAGES OF THE REVOCABLE LIVING TRUST

1. Initial *cost* and *trouble* of setup. Property must be transferred to the trust.

2. It slightly *complicates subsequent dealings* with the property.

3. It may require payment of an annual *trustee's fee* if someone besides yourself is trustee.

4. At time of termination, there may be *fees*.

5. There are no *immediate tax advantages*.

### Who Should Be Trustee?

You can be your own trustee, and couples can name themselves as trustees. The trust should provide for a successor trustee to take over in case you or both of you die or become incompetent. Your bank, a business friend, a relative, any of a number of persons can be named to serve as successor trustee. As the trust is revocable, and you can amend or modify it as long as you're alive and competent, you can change trustees, if things aren't going to suit you.

> *If I place property in a trust with a charity to pay me a return until I revoke the trust, or until I die, if I don't revoke it, can the charity use the trust property for its purposes until after I die?*

The trust property must be held for your benefit in this case and cannot be used by charity for its purposes until *after* you die.

> *If my trust is not managed well, can I sue the trustee?*

Practically anyone can sue anyone else in this sue-happy society in which we live, so the answer is yes. Whether you can collect, is another question.

The trustee is required to use at least the ordinary care and diligence which an ordinarily prudent person would use in the management of that person's own affairs, or in the care of that person's own property under similar circumstances. The law does not demand any more care than that.

It should be noted that, generally, the trustee takes the property placed in trust and invests and manages it. The beneficiary is paid a return from the trust property. If through unwise management, the trust property becomes worthless, then the beneficiary cannot look to other assets of the trustee to satisfy the terms of the trust. *This is true of all trusts,* assuming no breach of law or trust by the trustee.

> In 1925, Mr. Penberthy was made trustee of his nephew Homer's estate. He invested Homer's money in several properties. He also bought corporate bonds and some stock in a chain of clothing stores.
> When the depression of 1929 devasted the economy of

the country, the investments became worthless. Mr. Penberthy was not liable, for there was no way he could have foreseen such losses, nor could most men of ordinary prudence.

*Can't I use the one-page, fill-in-and-tear-out form I've heard about to do my own revocable living trust to solve my estate problems?*

Your trust must be properly prepared, implemented, and administered. We believe the one-page, do-it-yourself form of revocable living trust may cause you many more problems than it solves.

Now, let's look at the Irrevocable Living Trust.

## Chapter 13

# *More on Avoiding Probate Through Living Trusts*

### USE OF THE IRREVOCABLE LIVING TRUST
### IN AVOIDING PROBATE

If the trust agreement is irrevocable, it means just that. It can't be revoked (broken) except for the reasons given in Chapter 12.

Then, WHY would anyone WANT one?

There are always specific reasons for making an irrevocable trust agreement. Perhaps it involves a family business where some of the family members are getting on in years, and the family wants to make certain that management continues to run smoothly even if hindrances, such as senility, enter the picture.

Many times the reasons for an irrevocable trust involve estate and/or income tax avoidance. In order to be successful in such avoidance, the trustor must not have any direct or indirect power or control over the trust property or income. The regulations on this subject, set out in the Internal Revenue Code must be carefully followed.

One of the most popular living trusts used to avoid taxes is the *Irrevocable Charitable Remainder Trust*.

Rules concerning the use of this trust were set forth by the United States Congress in the Tax Reform Act of 1969, and in subsequent rulings and regulations. The terms of such trusts must be in strict compliance with all applicable provisions of the Internal Revenue Code and the regulations thereunder.

In order to gain tax benefits from use of the charitable remainder trust, the 1969 Tax Reform Act provides for three possible arrangements: (1) a Unitrust; (2) an Annuity Trust; (3) a Pooled Income Fund.

## Say That Again?

A *(Charitable Remainder) Unitrust* is a trust which is set up to pay a return or fixed annual percentage of 5 percent (or more) of the net fair market value of the assets placed in the trust. The trust assets are *revalued annually.* If the trust assets *appreciate,* the payment will increase. If they *depreciate,* the payment will *decrease.* Payments can come only from trust assets and income from same. If the assets are gone, payments stop. At death of the income beneficiary(-ies), all remaining trust assets go to your designated charity(-ies).

A *(Charitable Remainder) Annuity Trust* is a trust which is set up to pay a return or fixed annual percentage of 5 percent (or more) of the net fair market value of the assets placed in the trust. The trust assets are valued initially, at the time the property is placed in the trust. The trust assets are *never* revalued. Annual payments remain the same, whether the trust assets appreciate or depreciate. As in the unitrust, payments can come only from trust assets and income from same, and if the assets are gone, the payments stop. At death of the income beneficiary(-ies), all remaining assets go to your designated charity(-ies).

A *(Charitable Remainder) Pooled Income Fund* is an investment fund, much like a mutual fund. It is made up of transfers by many persons to the fund who receive *life income interest* in exchange for their transfers, based on the value of the transfer into the fund and based on the income earned by the fund. At death of the income beneficiary(-ies), the interest in the fund terminates and goes to named charity.

Again we stress the necessity of strict compliance with the Internal Revenue Code and regulations. This shouldn't frighten you away from use of one or more of these giving arrangements. They are very valuable and useful tools for those who set up the trust, as well as the beneficiaries.

In addition, the regulations assure, as much as possible, that charity will eventually be served. This was one of the main reasons *for* and accomplishments *of* the 1969 Tax Reform Act.

Now for an example of each of the Charitable Remainder Trusts.

### The Unclaimed Blessing Uses Strategy: Example #1—The Unitrust

Ruth has never been married and calls herself "an unclaimed blessing." She is sixty-three years old, has a good job, and lives alone in a rented apartment. She has stock which cost $2,700 originally and which is now valued at $22,500. She has $24,000 in two savings accounts, employee benefits including retirement, and Social Security when she retires, plus health and medical coverage.

Ruth's older sister is close, but her folks have passed on. The rest of her family are distant and very well off, materially speaking. She wants to remain independent for as long as she lives, but she wants her property to pass on her death without probate.

A friend told her about the *unitrust,* and he assisted her in making contact with the stewardship department of two of her favorite charities. (One of the charities sponsors children's orphanages in other countries, and the other ministers in the slums of several of our large cities.)

She liked what she saw. She put her stock in a *unitrust* with her college as trustee. She is to receive a 6 percent return per year for life, and at her death, the same income for her sister for *her* life. Then when both are dead, the remainder is to go to her college.

## No Taxes?

Because of the unitrust, even though the stock was valued at $22,500 and cost only $2,700 originally, *she paid no capital gain tax* (which she would have had to do if she kept the stock and sold it herself) and *she receives a return* on the $22,500 gift revalued annually.

She received a *present income tax deduction* computed on federal tax tables that consider her age, her sister's age, and the amount of the gift. Her deduction, in excess of $7,000, can be used at the rate of up to 50 percent of her gross income for the year in which the gift was made and for five succeeding years. As she is presently in the 38 percent income tax bracket, this will save her a lot of income tax.

## No Looking Back

The unitrust is irrevocable, and the property in the trust will belong to her college on death of Ruth and her sister without court administration or involvement.

Ruth would like this freedom from court administration with the rest of her property, but she doesn't want an irrevocable trust, because she may need the cash. Besides, she wants use of her furniture and personal things during her life.

## Clever Thinking

Therefore, she made a *revocable trust agreement* with herself as trustee. The trust includes $14,000 of her savings, her furniture, and personal property. The charity that sponsors children's orphanages is named as the successor trustee at her death or court adjudicated incapacity (if the Court finds her incapable or incompetent of administering her affairs).

The successor trustee is instructed to pay her debts from the trust assets, as well as arrange and pay for her funeral. All property that remains after debts and funeral are paid will belong to the charity.

Ruth can *revoke* this trust and have use of part or all of the property during her life.

## There's More?

She also set up a *Totten Trust* with her second savings account of $10,000 naming herself as trustee, and the charity that ministers in city slums as trust beneficiary. The *Totten Trust,* also called *Bank Trust,* is where a person deposits money in a bank account in the person's own name as trustee for a beneficiary. The trust is revocable in whole or part by the depositor—that is, the depositor can take out funds from the account—unless the gift is completed in life by delivering the bankbook or the money to the beneficiary, or on the death of the depositor, in which case the remaining funds go to the beneficiary. Some use this trust arrangement instead of placing their funds in a joint tenancy account.

Ruth has access to these funds, but they will go to the charity on her death.

Under the present circumstances, Ruth will have no estate at her death which will require probate, and there will be no taxes to pay.

## The Leftovers

Though Ruth used both revocable and irrevocable living trusts, it was also recommended to her that there be a "Catch All" or "Pour Over" will to act upon and pass any property that may, for one reason or another, not be covered by the trust agreement or agreements. She now has her will and the arrangements she has made will provide for her sister, her interests, and herself.

Your local law should be checked on the use and effect of these trusts in your area.

## In Case You're Wondering

### *What happens to Ruth's trusts for a charity if the charity goes out of business?*

Your trustee is authorized to name a substitute, if that is the sole charity. Most people name several charities with instructions to distribute to those that are still in business and qualify under Internal Revenue regulations at the time of the distribution.

## Jack Be Nimble: Example #2—The Annuity Trust

Jack had gone through the depression of the thirties and knew that the market didn't always go up. He debated for

a long time as to whether he would put his money in a *gift annuity* or a *charitable remainder annuity trust.* (See Chapter 10 for an explanation of gift annuity.)

Finally, he decided on the *annuity trust,* which pegged his income on the initial net fair market value of the assets he placed in the trust. These assets *would not be revalued down,* and *his payment would not be reduced if his trust assets went down in value.* Jack realized he could only look to the trust assets and income from those trust assets for his payment, but he didn't mind that.

Besides the income payments to Jack, he received an immediate income tax deduction. Also, none of the assets will be in his estate at his death to be taxed.

### Into the Pool: Example #3—The Pooled Income Fund

Priscilla thought she wanted a *charitable remainder unitrust.* She spoke to the stewardship representative of her church about it, mentioning that she wanted her money to go to the church at her death. Priscilla had been recently widowed, and the funds she had to invest were relatively

small. So the representative recommended that, instead of a unitrust, she put $4,000 in a Charitable Remainder Pooled Income Fund, set up and administered by the church.

Besides the income payments from her portion of the fund, she will receive an immediate income tax deduction and none of the assets will be in her estate at the time of her death to be taxed.

### Should I name a charity as trustee of my charitable remainder trust?

This is often done if the organization is qualified to so act under local law. The organization's representatives can satisfy you in that regard. Often they will serve without fee, which is an additional incentive.

## ADVANTAGES OF AN IRREVOCABLE LIVING TRUST

1. You *see* your trust *work*.
2. You *observe your trustee* in action.
3. You *avoid probate* and *court costs*.
4. You probably will *save* some *fees*.
5. It's a good way to pass property to *charity*.
6. You *save any taxes* there may be on the property going to charity at your death.
7. With irrevocable charitable remainder trusts, created while you are living, you can get an *income tax deduction* during your life.
8. You can *save capital gain taxes* on property placed in a charitable remainder trust and receive income on the appreciated value.

## DISADVANTAGES OF AN IRREVOCABLE LIVING TRUST

1. Property must be transferred, so there is *initial cost* and *effort* in setting up the trust.
2. You *lose all control* over the property with most irrevocable trusts.
3. It requires *annual* fiduciary *accounting* and possible *tax returns*.

   4. It may require payment of annual *trustee fees*.
   5. There may be *fees* at time of trust termination.
   6. You *can't change your mind* and get the property back.

## That's Just the Beginning

We haven't mentioned many of the "Trust Products" available. But a few of interest might be:

*Short Term Clifford Trust* used by those in high income brackets to save income taxes.

*Sprinkling Trust* used to provide for the payment of income and/or principal among two or more beneficiaries within the discretion of the trustee.

*Grandfather Trust* used by grandparents to serve their grandchildren and others.

*Insurance Trust* used by many to provide for family support and freedom from want, usually in case of the death of the breadwinner and other purposes as well.

*Charitable Lead Trust* for those in high federal gift and estate tax brackets.

## Many Have Asked About—

*Pure Equity Funding Trust* used for an arrangement of assets which is called by some promoters the *Family Estate, Family Trust,* or *Pure Equity Trust*. Purportedly, it is used by the rich (but promoted for the use of the not-so-rich) to avoid paying taxes, protect against creditors and lawsuits, and assure a life of ease and privacy to the user.

Although the titles of this arrangement sound good (for they mimic the perfectly acceptable titles and arrangements of family trusts that we have described on other pages of this book), the arrangement itself is suspect.

It is likely that you'll recognize the difference between it and the acceptable family trust, though, for those who promote various forms of this creation puff their products to be the end of any concerns or worries you might have about future taxes, creditors, and so forth.

The Internal Revenue Service and the Federal Tax Courts have been involved in a crackdown regarding phases of this arrangement, so you should discuss this matter in detail with your own attorney before deciding to make a form of this trust a part of your estate plan.

### It's Here to Stay

A comprehensive work on trusts would more than fill this book because once you've set forth as many as you can find, then you can start mixing them to serve your purposes in an almost infinite variety of ways.

Needless to say, the trust is here to stay and is a very valuable and useful estate-planning tool, if competently prepared, implemented, and used to serve your purposes. We repeat: A one-page, do-it-yourself, fill-in-the-blanks form is NOT the answer, but an invitation to trouble. The person who chooses the trust as an estate-planning vehicle is well advised to seek and follow professional advice as to its preparation and use.

**Chapter 14**

# The Economic Recovery Tax Act of 1981—Bugaboo or Blessing?

The Economic Recovery Tax Act of 1981, signed by President Reagan on August 13, 1981, has been labeled by many as the largest tax cut in history. It makes sweeping changes in the taxes for individuals and for business.

The estate planner has had to adjust to a whole new world. There are over a hundred changes that apply to taxpayers in almost every bracket, for this new law is not only for the rich. It is a law that affects and can benefit everyone.

**Caution**

Some of the benefits are not automatic, and some of the changes can act to penalize the unwary and those who are satisfied with the status quo, rather than take advantage of this new law.

For example, as we stated in a previous chapter, the Act allows spouses to transfer between themselves unlimited amounts of assets (other than certain terminable interests, which we'll later explain) without federal estate or gift tax liability.

This means, if Ed has a million-dollar or a ten-million-dollar estate, he can give it all to his wife Anna and have no federal gift tax during his life, or if he does this by a will, living trust, insurance beneficiary designation, or other means at his death, his estate will have no *federal* estate tax to pay. If there is no gift or death or inheritance tax in Ed's *state,* then there will be *no* tax on the passing of this property from Ed to Anna.

HOWEVER, on Anna's death, the chickens come home to roost, as we used to say in Montana. Anna's estate may be liable for a huge tax at that point, which could have been reduced or even avoided if Ed and Anna had done some estate tax planning before Ed died. Of course, Anna had several tax-savings options available to her after Ed died, but not nearly as many as when both Ed and Anna were living.

If the expansion of tax breaks already in our laws and the creation of new tax breaks are regarded by you as a blessing, then this new law (referred to hereafter as *the Act)* is a blessing!

> **Note:** Since this law has to do with federal gift and estate tax, we will not repeat the word "federal" hereafter, in every instance, and we will make no allowance for state death taxes or credits in the cases discussed.

**For Openers**

The Act makes income-tax cuts across the board, it changes the rules as they apply to long-term capital gains, and it provides favorable changes for the self-employed covered under HR-10 (Keogh) plans. It reduces the marriage tax penalty incurred by husband and wife where both spouses work, file joint returns, and end up paying more combined tax than two single people who make the same total wages, but file separately.

It deals with the alternate minimum tax, and it increases the amount that can be deducted for child care.

The Act increases to two years (from 18 months) the period

within which you can sell a residence and buy another more expensive residence and postpone paying tax on some or all of the gain from the sale. Furthermore, it increases from $100,000 to $125,000 the once-in-a-lifetime exclusion of taxable gain on sale of a residence for individuals fifty-five years of age or older, and who have used the property as a principal residence for at least three out of the last five years preceding the year of sale.

All property in your estate is taxed based upon its fair market value, but in order to permit a continuation of family farms and ownership of real property used in closely held businesses, the law allows a special valuation for this property at less than the fair market value, providing certain regulations are complied with. The purpose of this special valuation law is to prevent the need to sell these properties in order to pay taxes. The Act liberalizes the rules that apply to these operations.

*There are entire books or sets of books describing the new laws, some of which are referred to for your information in our bibliography.*

For our purposes, we will deal only with a few which are essential to proper estate planning and concentrate on a part of the Act that deals with "Estate and Gift Tax" as it affects the estate plan and planner.

### Federal Estate Tax—What Is It?

The federal estate tax is a tax assessed on your property when you die. If your total estate (cash, buildings, stock, jewelry, cars, life insurance—yes, believe it or not, life insurance proceeds—etc.) at your death is more than the amount the government says is exempt from tax, then the amount of the estate, less the exemption stated in the Act and less deductions, is taxed starting at 32% in 1982 and going up as high as 60% in 1983. The *maximum* gift and estate tax rates are reduced by the Act so that the 70% maximum tax under the old law will be reduced in steps from 1982 to 1985, and so that the maximum tax in 1985 and after will be 50%. (See the upcoming chart for the yearly progression of this benefit.)

**More Good News**
There are a variety of allowable deductions that can be added to the exemption, stated in the Act, including the unlimited marital deduction (between spouses only), deductions for funeral costs, administration expenses, valid claims against the estate, and the unlimited deduction for charitable gifts.

One method we've found used by many people over the years to reduce their taxable estate creates problems and does little for tax savings. This method is the gifting or transfer of property where the giver retains the control over or use of the property for life. This property will generally be included in your taxable estate at the time of your death.

The laws governing estate and gift taxes have gone through a period of radical changes in just these last few years.

Prior to 1976  Federal estate tax exemption was $60,000, so all estates over $60,000 were subject to estate tax. There was also a $30,000 lifetime gift tax exemption, plus you could make any number of $3,000 per person gifts per year, and these were exempt from tax.

In 1976  Congress changed the $60,000 Federal estate tax exemption and eliminated the $30,000 lifetime gift tax exemption and instituted in their place the **UNIFIED CREDIT.** This meant that your total gifts over $3,000 per person each year, plus the amount of your estate at death would be exempt from federal estate tax up to the amount of the exemption in any one year. This exemption started at $120,000 in 1977 and increased each year until 1981, when it became $175,625.

## To Make It Clearer

| If a person died in | The Unified Credit Would Be | The Estate Which Could Pass Without Federal Estate Tax (i.e. The Exemption Equivalent Was |
|---|---|---|
| 1977 | $30,000 | $120,666 |
| 1978 | $34,000 | $134,000 |
| 1979 | $38,000 | $147,333 |
| 1980 | $42,500 | $161,563 |
| 1981 | $47,000 | $175,625 |

In 1981   This same unified credit exemption equivalent plan was followed, but the figures were increased eventually by over 400%, so that . . .

| If a person died in | The Unified Credit Would Be | The Estate Which Could Pass Without Federal Estate Tax (i.e., The Exemption Equivalent) is |
|---|---|---|
| 1982 | $ 63,800 | $225,000 |
| 1983 | $ 79,300 | $275,000 |
| 1984 | $ 96,300 | $325,000 |
| 1985 | $121,800 | $400,000 |
| 1986 | $155,800 | $500,000 |
| 1987 | $192,800 | $600,000 |

Please Note:

1. The maximum gift and estate tax rates under prior law were 70%. The Act reduced the rates to 50% in 1985. But the Tax Reform Act of 1984 retains 55% as the maximum rate through 1987 when it will reduce to a maximum of 50%.
2. Your estate will need to file a federal estate tax return when you die only if your estate exceeds the exemption equivalent on the date of your death.

### Thanks, Uncle Sam

Prior to 1981, the Exemption Equivalent would be reduced by the total of gifts made in excess of $3,000 per person per year. The Act increased the gift exclusion to $10,000 per person per year on all gifts made after 1981. Now you can make as many gifts of $10,000 per person per year as you like and not use up any of your lifetime exemption. A married couple can give $20,000 per person per year without using up any of the lifetime exemption each has. For gifts made after 1981 in excess of the $10,000 exclusion, gift tax returns are to be filed, and any payment of gift tax is to be paid by April 15 following the close of the calendar year in which the gifts are made.

### Even More Good News

The Act allows an unlimited estate tax marital deduction. That is, spouses can transfer unimited amounts to each other during lifetime or at death without tax liability. (Note: Discuss with your attorney, CPA, or other adviser the basic problems that can arise from so-called death-bed transfer or transfers that return to the donor within one year of the date of the gift.)

### Another Change

The Act also allows certain trusts to qualify for the marital deduction called "Qualified Terminable Interest Property Trusts" or QTIP Trusts. This trust arrangement permits a spouse to give to the surviving spouse an income interest and certain other benefits in the deceased spouse's property for the life of the surviving spouse, but gives the deceased spouse the right to direct where the property is to go when the surviving spouse dies. Thus the deceased spouse can care for the surviving spouse but can at the death of the surviving spouse provide for the children and/or grandchildren, friends, relatives, charity, or whatever. When the surviving spouse dies, the balance in this QTIP trust is added to the surviving spouse's estate in determining the amount of federal estate taxes.

We'll discuss this trust in more detail later in the chapter.

## LET'S SEE HOW SOME OF THE VARIOUS PLANS NOW POSSIBLE COMPARE TO EACH OTHER IN ACTUAL USE

### FIRST CASE

Dan and Betty have done no estate planning. Their children have left home, are married and independent, and have presented Dan and Betty with three grandchildren.

Dan and Betty have an estate valued at $440,000. Dan will retire in three years, at which time the insurance he has with his company of $50,000 will terminate, reducing their estate to $390,000. They hold their property, including their $140,000 home, in joint tenancy.

They want to tithe their estate when both have died and have the balance go to the children and grandchildren.

### SUGGESTED PLAN

Dan and Betty should have a will or living trust which provides that everything go to the survivor on the death of the first, and on the death of both, 10% to their favorite charities, including their church, and 90% outright in equal shares to their living children. Their plan should include provision for the possibility that a child of theirs would be dead and leave living children (Don and Betty's grandchildren), and the share of the dead child would then be administrered and distributed in a trust for the benefit of those grandchildren.

### TAX ON THIS PLAN
#### First Death

| | |
|---|---|
| $440,000 | Amount of estate—assume death of Dan 1984 |
| $440,000 | To Betty |
| - 0 - | Federal estate tax on first to die = NONE |

#### Second Death

| | |
|---|---|
| $440,000 | Amount of estate on death of Betty— assume 1985 (no increase or decrease of estate) |
| − $ 44,000 | To charity = deduction |
| $396,000 | Taxable estate to children |
| − $400,000 | Exemption Equivalent in 1985 |
| - 0 - | Federal estate tax = NONE |

It was pointed out to Dan and Betty that if Dan died in 1984, did no tax planning, and simply passed all of the estate to Betty by will, living trust, joint tenancy survivorship, insurance beneficiary designation, or other means, and Betty died later in 1984, her estate would have an exemption of only $325,000, plus their gift to charity, leaving federal tax to be paid of approximately $25,000. They preferred to take the chance that one of them would live until 1985 or after, when the exemption would increase and make tax planning unnecessary.

## SECOND CASE

When Al and Dorothy came to me the plan they had set up was a blueprint for disaster. They have an estate of a little over $1,300,000, including $200,000 of life insurance on Al's life. They had a simple will leaving everything to each other, and Al's insurance named Dorothy as beneficiary. They have four children, ages 6, 8, 12, and 15, and on death of both their estate was to be given to their children for whom they named guardians.

## THEIR PLAN AS IT WAS ORIGINALLY

### *First Death*

| | |
|---|---|
| $1,300,000 | Amount of estate after costs—assume death of Al 1987 |
| $1,300,000 | To Dorothy, using unlimited marital deduction |
| - 0 - | Federal estate tax on first death—NONE |

### *Second Death*

| | |
|---|---|
| $1,300,000 | Amount of estate after costs except taxes—assume death of Dorothy 1989 (no increase of estate) |
| − $ 600,000 | Exemption Equivalent |
| $ 700,000 | Taxable estate |
| − $ 278,000 | Federal estate tax |
| $ 422,000 | Estate |
| $1,022,000 | Estate after costs and Federal tax |

The total estate of $1,022,000 which would go to the children was to be divided into four equal shares, or $255,500 each.

Assuming the children would be 12, 14, 18, and 21 years of age when Dorothy died, the 18-year-old and the 21-year-old each would receive $255,500 free of any control or restriction. Can you imagine the trouble a half-million dollars can buy?

The shares of the two younger children would be held by their guardians in rigidly and expensively managed accounts. The court would, on petition from the guardian, prepared by an attorney, tell the guardian what could and what could not be paid out of those accounts. And here again, as the child attained the age of eighteen, the money would have to be given to the child—no holds barred, and all of this after paying the government $278,000 in taxes, which could have been avoided.

## THE NEW PLAN

Al and Dorothy decided they had to do tax and family planning to avert the disaster, so they chose a revocable living trust, which avoids all court involvement on the death of either or both of them.

Their plan provides that, on the death of the first of them to die, their estate will be split, and on the side of the one who dies first will be placed, in a separate trust, the largest amount that will be free of federal estate tax. This amount and the remainder of the estate will all be available to the survivor. While both are alive they serve as trustees of their trust, and when one dies, the survivor serves as sole trustee. They name successor trustees to take over at the death or incapacity of both. They decide there is more than enough to take care of the children, and so they want a tithe or 10% of their entire estate to go to charity. If both die, they have their property remain in trust for the children, with separate shares to care for the needs and education of each child and distribution of the remaining principal: ⅓ to be received by each child at age 25, ⅓ at age 30, and the balance at age 35. Furthermore, the trust makes provision for grandchildren.

## TAX ON THIS PLAN

### First Death

| | |
|---|---|
| $1,300,000 | Estate after costs—assume death of Al in 1987 |
| − $ 600,000 | Into Exemption Equivalent Trust to care for Dorothy for life, then out to children and grandchildren |
| $ 700,000 | To survivor's marital trust for Dorothy without restriction as to use |
| - 0 - | Federal estate tax—NONE |

### Second Death

| | |
|---|---|
| $ 700,000 | Estate after costs—assume death of Dorothy in 1989 (no increase or decrease in amount of estate)  Note: $600,000 in exemption equivalent trust not included in Dorothy's estate as it is sheltered and goes to the children and/or grandchildren free of federal estate tax. |
| − $ 130,000 | Tithe of original estate to charity = deduction |
| $ 570,000 | Taxable estate after charitable deduction |
| − $ 600,000 | Exemption Equivalent |
| - 0 - | Federal estate tax—NONE |

With this plan and under these circumstances, there is no federal estate tax to pay. Probate and substantial court fees, additional expense, and delays are avoided, and the total estate after costs is available to benefit the children and grandchildren and also charity.

## QTIP Again

There are a variety of different ways Al and Dorothy could have completed their planning. They could have utilized the Qualified Terminable Interest Property Trust (mentioned earlier), which, at death of the first spouse to die, can assure the first to die that he or she will have control of the ultimate distribution of the remainder of his or her estate on the death of the second to die.

A terminable interest is defined in IRC Section 2056(b)(1) as an interest that may fail on the lapse of time or on the occurrence or failure to occur of an event or contingency. This means if a person provides for an interest in his or her estate to go to a spouse, which interest is terminable, then that interest is included in the estate of the giver and does not qualify for the marital deduction. This rule, however, does not apply to the "Qualified Terminable Interest Property" Trust.

When a spouse makes provision for the "Qualified Terminable Interest" to go to the surviving spouse at the death of the first to die, that interest is not taxed in the estate of the first to die, and only what is left of it when the survivor dies is included in the estate of the second to die, for tax purposes.

### Let's See How It Works

### THIRD CASE

Ted and Judy have an estate of $900,000, but as Ted's computer business is very successful, he expects the estate will be substantially larger than that when he dies. Ted and Judy have a problem many have in our society. Judy is Ted's second wife and twenty years younger than he. They have no children from this marriage, but Ted has three adult children by his first marriage. Ted and Judy are very much in love. Judy has helped him acquire this successful business. Yet Judy is young and very attractive, and Ted is concerned that if he dies and leaves the entire estate to Judy, she might get involved in another marriage, and his children might not eventually receive a fair share of the estate.

### SUGGESTED PLAN

Ted and Judy discussed their problem freely with me as

their attorney. I suggested that they utilize an estate-splitting tax-savings trust, i.e., an Exemption Equivalent Trust, as did Al and Dorothy, but that, in addition, they also consider a Qualified Terminable Interest Property Trust (QTIP).

This could be accomplished either with a will and testamentary trusts, requiring probate, or a revocable living trust which avoids probate. Ted and Judy chose the will and testamentary trust, though an increasing percentage of clients are opting in favor of the revocable living trust.

The wills of Ted and Judy are very similar. As all of their assets are community property, when one dies, the survivor will have his or her one-half of the estate outright and free of trust. The will specifies where the survivor's property is to go, with a part going to charity and the balance going to family, to include children, grandchildren, parents, and so forth. The one-half of the estate that belongs to the first to die will be divided into two trusts. One trust, being the Exemption Equivalent Trust, will have in it property with a value equal to the amount of the Exemption Equivalent in the year of the death of the first to die. This will vary according to the chart previously explained in this chapter.

The balance of the one-half of the estate of the first to die will go into a separate trust for the benefit of the surviving spouse for life, but at the death of the surviving spouse this property will go out to the beneficiaries named by the first to die. Judy has relatives and friends she wants to benefit besides Ted's children, whom she considers her own, but Ted has his children and grandchildren take the remaining property from both the Exemption Equivalent Trust and the Qualified Terminable Interest Property Trust (QTIP) after Judy has died.

## What Does It Look Like?

Assume Ted dies first, in 1985, and the total estate now is $1,100,000 after costs:

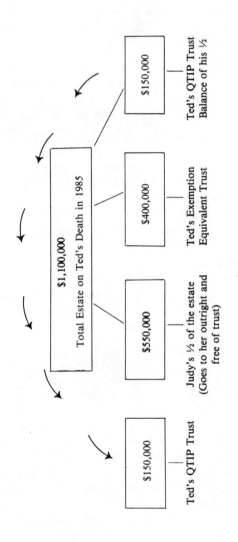

1. There is no federal estate tax on Ted's death.
2. From Judy's one-half she can . . .
   a. Live on it
   b. Give it away
   c. Invest and use it as she sees fit
3. From Ted's Exemption Equivalent Trust . . .
   a. Judy is Trustee and Ted gives her
      1) Net income for life
      2) Principal if she needs it, (NOTE TO ATTORNEYS: with an ascertainable standard)
      3) 5% or $5,000 a year, whichever is greater, without regard to need

Note: Ted could have given Judy additional benefits from this trust, but they decided that, at Judy's death, Ted's will should provide that whatever is left in the equivalent trust will go to Ted's children, with provisions for Ted's grandchildren. (This trust estate will pass to the children or grandchildren without federal estate tax, even though the original $400,000 estate may have grown considerably larger by the time Judy dies.)

4. From Ted's Qualified Terminable Interest Property Trust, Judy is trustee and Ted gives her net income for life.

Note: Ted could have given her additional benefits such as power to invade principal, as in the other trust, as well as other benefits, but both Ted and Judy decided against this so Ted could rest assured his children and grandchildren will receive 80% of what is left of the property after Judy dies, and Ted's favorite charities will receive 20%.

5. Whereas on Judy's death there will be no federal estate tax on Ted's Exemption Equivalent Trust, whatever is left of Judy's one-half and Ted's QTIP Trust will be added together. Then after deducting costs, any provision for charity, and the Exemption Equivalent in the year of Judy's death, a federal estate tax must be paid on the balance.

Assume Judy dies in 1995 and her estate of $550,000 has grown to $700,000 and Ted's QTIP Trust has grown to $300,000. Judy, in her will, has given 50% of her estate to Ted's children and grandchildren, 30% to her parents and brothers and sisters, and 20% to her church and other charities. As stated before, Ted provided that 80% of whatever was left of his QTIP Trust on Judy's death would go to his children and grandchildren, and 20% would go to charity.

| | | |
|---:|---:|---|
| $ | 700,000 | Amount of estate after costs and before taxes—assume Judy's death in 1995 |
| + | 300,000 | Ted's QTIP Trust—amount assumed after costs and before taxes |
| | $1,000,000 | Total Judy's estate and QTIP Trust |
| − | 600,000 | Judy's Exemption Equivalent |
| $ | 400,000 | Taxable estate |
| − | 140,000 | To charity per Judy's will |
| $ | 260,000 | Taxable estate |
| − | 60,000 | To charity per Ted's will from his QTIP Trust |
| $ | 200,000 | Estate to be taxed |
| $ | 75,000 | Federal estate tax |

Altogether Ted's children and grandchildren and Judy's relatives will receive $725,000 from Judy's Exemption Equivalent and the $125,000 left after taxes. In addition, Ted's children and grandchildren receive, without federal estate tax, the entire balance of Ted's Exemption Equivalent Trust which had in it, at the time of Ted's death, the sum of $325,000. Of course, by the time of Judy's death, that amount could be considerably larger.

Also, $200,000 is available for charity from Judy's estate and Ted's QTIP Trust. Only $75,000 is paid out for federal estate tax on Ted and Judy's rather sizable estate, due largely to Ted and Judy's wisdom in completing their planning. Had they failed to do this planning, the tax bite would have been substantially larger.

And then, Judy has several options available to her, such as gifting to her loved ones or placing property in revocable trusts with charities, *all of which could easily eliminate taxes altogether,* while Judy remained independent for as long as she lived.

## An Added Benefit

The QTIP Trust can also be utilized by married couples to accomplish much of what planners used to have to accomplish with the unitrust, annuity trust, or pooled income fund trust. (See Chapter 13.)

The amount of property set aside for the use of the surviving spouse in a QTIP trust is free of federal estate tax at the death of the first spouse to die, as it qualifies as a part of the marital deduction.

The surviving spouse can then use this property for as long as he or she lives, but then the first to die can provide in his or her will or living trust that when the surviving spouse dies, the amount left in the QTIP trust will go to charity. This amount will then be a charitable deduction from the total estate to be taxed on the death of the surviving spouse. The parties may want to serve their church or other charity this way while at the same time having use of all of their estate while either is alive, and this will accomplish what they wish in a very effective way.

## Caution

If you have a tax-savings trust that was signed prior to September 12, 1981, it is very important that you have this checked and probably amended to take advantage of the new law. Probably the words "maximum marital deduction" appear in your tax-savings trust. Under the prior-to-the-Act law this meant one-half of your estate or $250,000, whichever was greater, whereas those words now mean all of your estate. If you don't amend your document made prior to September 12, 1981, the prior-to-the-Act law may apply, unless your state legislature enacts law allowing you advantages under the new law. (Check this with your counsel.)

But please remember this. As you have read this chapter, you may realize you don't want either the old or the new meaning of the words "maximum marital deduction" to apply to your estate plan, but a plan whereby you place as much of your estate in your sheltered tax-savings trust as can go in any one year tax free, with the balance of the estate to go to your spouse—*all of it tax free on the death of the first of you to die, but with the additional benefit of less to be taxed, than before the Act, on the second of you to die.* Some say, "This is the greatest benefit to come our way since the discovery of the wheel."

The Economic Recovery Tax Act of 1981—Bugaboo? or Blessing?—Surely a blessing for *almost* everyone.

## More Thoughts on Taxes in General

### *What is the difference between Federal Estate Tax and inheritance, succession, or death tax?*

The Federal Estate Tax is the tax levied by the United States on your taxable estate based upon its value at your date of death, or on an alternate valuation date six months after death, or on date of distribution, if sooner than six months. Your estate, called your "Gross Estate," will consist of everything you own at the time of your death. In order to arrive at your net taxable estate, there are certain allowable deductions, such as funeral and last illness expenses, debts, costs of administration, marital deduction, and property given to charity, as well as others.

The tax is then computed, and a tax credit, as discussed in the preceding pages, is deducted from the computed figure to arrive at the tax to be paid.

All of the states, except for Nevada, charge what is called a *death tax,* a *succession tax, inheritance tax,* and/or a *pick-up tax,* depending upon which state you are in. The result is the same. The state receives tax from your estate, as does the Federal Government. Subject to certain limitations, a credit is allowed against the Federal Tax due, for a portion—and sometimes all—of the state tax paid. The inheritance tax is usually scaled up or down depending upon the relationship of the person receiving to the person giving. A spouse pays the least tax, the children the next least, and on down through other relatives until it eventually comes to people with no blood relationship to the person giving.

California voters have recently abolished the inheritance tax, and this has been accomplished in other states as well.

However, even states which have no estate or inheritance tax as such, except for Nevada, receive a part of the tax assessed to your estate by the federal government, in the form of what is called the pick-up tax.

### How long after death does my estate have to pay taxes?

The estate has nine months from your death to pay the Federal Estate Tax. But in order to reduce the need of forcing a sale of estate assets to pay the taxes, the 1976 Tax Reform Act and the Economic Recovery Tax Act of 1981 have liberalized some old provisions and added some new ones to our laws. Now, if a "reasonable cause" can be established for deferring payment, the Internal Revenue Service can grant reasonable periods of time up to ten years within which to pay the federal tax and, in certain instances (for example, involving a closely held business) the extension to pay the tax can total fifteen years.

Regarding state tax, you should check out the current time to pay and extension provisions in effect in your state, with local counsel.

The wise estate planner, however, will not depend on extension provisions, but will plan sufficient liquidity in an estate, falling back on the extension provisions only in case of an emergency.

### Whose business is it what I do with my possessions? Didn't I already pay income tax on everything I have?

Whether we like it or not, we have little control over the tax laws that are passed, though more and more people realize they can make changes, as is the case recently in California, where people voted inheritance taxes out of existence. If, however, the law says your estate must pay tax, then the tax must be paid. There are many ways to avoid or reduce those taxes through advance planning, but that's up to you. When you go to the polls next time, remember to vote against those who support government policies that insist on setting up one expensive program after another that must be supported by additional taxes. Just complaining about the tax won't take it away.

No, we can't avoid death and we have a problem with taxes. You need to do what you can to make both problems easier to face for you and your loved ones. You don't want to be so concerned about taxes, however, that you deprive yourself and go without. You have only one life to live. There is no sense in refusing to enjoy any of your assets just so your heirs will be left with plenty of money. Sometimes, that's the worst thing you can do to them.

# Chapter 15

# *What About the Second Marriage*

Jan's husband died in the war. Jan received a number of benefits from the government, as did their four children. Their house was hers, free of debt. When she fell in love with Tom, five years later, her only thought was "We'll be together forever!

She placed everything in joint tenancy with him even though he brought nothing into their marriage except his two children and some bills from his deceased wife's lengthy illness.

Their few years of marriage were beautiful. Then tragedy struck! Jan contracted leukemia and died. All of her property held in joint tenancy passed to Tom. A year later, tragedy struck again! Tom was struck down with a heart attack and passed away in his sleep. He had left no will.

Now, the question was, who would be given the property that Tom received from Jan? And who would be given the property they had acquired together during their marriage?

Each of the fifty states gives its own answers to these questions. The rules of intestate succession had to be applied to Tom's estate. That is, the estate was distributed as the state felt best. It probably was not the way Jan and Tom would have wanted it. Furthermore, the property that passed was reduced by a lot of fees and costs. (See Chapter 5, "Why Not Just Let It Happen?")

Whether remarriage follows death or divorce, both parties should consider estate planning to take care of their new circumstances and responsibilities, as a Number One priority. One fellow stated:

> *My wife and I have our own separate property from prior marriages. We desire that the property go to our respective children by these former marriages. We both have wills to this effect, executed before our present marriage. Should the wills be updated?*

Yes. Both of you should make new wills or amend the old ones by codicil just as soon as possible. The laws of the various states differ as to the rights you have to each other's property.

But you should not leave this for the law to resolve, perhaps after expensive court litigation. This should be the subject of a new estate plan. You and your wife should provide for what is to be done with all your properties, separate or otherwise, so that both of you and your children will be served properly. Your attorney can show you what you can and must do in this regard.

### Preparing for Change

> *My wife and I have provided that all of our property is to go to the survivor, and on the death of the survivor, to our children. If the survivor remarries, what happens to our plan to provide for the children with our estate?*

The problem is not a difficult one to solve. Most people trust their mates in their absence to do what is best for the children with their mutual property.

If you wish to make provision concerning it now, however, you can do it with a separate contract between you and your wife, or you can place your part of the property in a trust for use of your wife for her life and then out to the children.

## How to Serve Them Both

*I have a daughter by a predeceased wife. I want
my daughter to eventually have my home after
my present wife and I are dead. How may I do
what is best for both my wife and daughter?*

You can place your home in a *trust* during your lifetime, or
in your *will*, providing use of it by your wife for life with the
stipulation that it will pass on to your daughter at your wife's
death. Or you can will a *life estate* in the property to your
wife, with the property to go to your daughter when your
wife dies. However, there are many problems with the con-
ventional life estate, such as who repairs and maintains the
property, who insures it, who pays taxes and assessments,
and so forth. Use of the trust will eliminate these problems
and still accomplish what you wish.

## Making Sure

*Is the antenuptial agreement something that
should be considered in a second marriage?*

Such a consideration would be wise for many. The
popularity of such an agreement seems to be increasing.
Basically, an antenuptial agreement is something like this:

Charles and Carolyn, in planning marriage, have expressed their concern regarding their separate estates.
Charles' assets amount to nearly $900,000 and Carolyn's
approximately $500,000. Both have children from former
marriages.

They have decided to draw up an antenuptial agreement,
under which the rights to the property of each other are
spelled out, including what happens in case of death or
divorce.

## The Merry Widow

*I'm a widow with some separate property.
What happens to my separate property if I
remarry? Does it automatically belong to my
new spouse?*

No. Your separate property remains your separate property until you do something to change it. (See Chapter 11 for a definition of separate property.)

## House to Spouse?

*I received a house in a divorce settlement. Would it go to my present spouse if I die without a will?*

If you've made no arrangement to avoid probate, and you die without a will, your house will go in accordance with the laws of intestate succession in effect in your state at the time of your death. (See Chapter 5.)

Your husband, your children, your grandchildren, parents, brothers, sisters, or others, may receive a part of your house, depending upon what living relatives you have.

Don't do this to yourself, your loved ones, or your estate. Plan before you die for an orderly passing of your property to whomever you want to have it.

There are various ways your house can pass at your death without being covered by a will, of course. (See Chapters 10 through 13.)

## Similar But Different

*When I die, will my ex-husband be able to collect any of my estate?*

No, except he may be able to benefit indirectly from property going to your minor children or in satisfaction of a debt you may owe him.

## When There's Bitterness

*My wife and I are divorced. The court gave her custody of our child. Does this give her the right to name a guardian when she dies, contrary to my wishes?*

The statutes of the various states differ on the rights of

parents in their will to appoint a third person as guardian, instead of the surviving parent. You should check your local statutes.

In California, when one parent dies, the surviving parent normally has the right to be guardian of the *person* of the child, but a parent can appoint a third person as guardian of the *property* being left the child, in event of the death of that parent.

> ### One of the reasons I divorced my husband was his neglect of the children. Would he receive custody if I die?

In a divorce, the Court decides who will receive custody of children, and in some instances, where both parents are still living and are considered unfit, takes the children away from those parents, makes them wards of the Court, and places them with relatives or in a foster home. If, after you die, it can be shown to the satisfaction of the Court that the children's father is incapable of serving as custodian or guardian, by reason of unfitness, then the Court will find someone else to take care of them. In the absence of proof of unfitness, the children's father will receive their custody.

## Chapter 16

# *When You Have Been Left Behind*

If it is of any comfort to you, I know what it's like.

The Montana spring air had begun to turn the ice and snow to slush. My Dad, who never seemed to become ill, had come home from work early, not feeling well. The doctor couldn't diagnose what was wrong, but the high fever spelled trouble.

We children were taken to Grandma's and told to pray for Dad. The hours dragged—the news was not good. And then came word: Dad's dead. Blood poisoning from a scratch. Five days from strapping health to death.

When we were allowed to see Mom, she was lying on the bed in the guest room, crying. My Aunt Adele whispered to me, "You're going to have to be the man of the house now, George." A thirteen-year-old boy, the oldest of three children, the man of the house? I didn't WANT to be the man of the house. I wanted my Dad back—and so did my Mom. But now she had to be Mom *and* Dad to two little children and her thirteen-year-old son who was to be her "man of the house."

What precious memories I have of that brave little lady, turning our home into a photo studio. Together, we built backgrounds and camera tripods out of wood. We fashioned a darkroom in the basement and had a little gift shop in the front room where Mom displayed and sold works of art she produced in the night hours, long after we had gone to bed.

We watched her, worked with her, prayed with her,

cried with her, and loved her, but we couldn't know her heartaches—the loneliness of being without her husband and lover of fifteen years.

Since that time long ago, I've worked with a great many widowed persons, and I've become more and more convinced that few people can appreciate the trauma that comes in the aftermath of the death of a mate, unless they have experienced it themselves. Part of that trauma is supplied by business decisions that have to be made.

Questions like these haunt the bereaved:

> *Now that my spouse is gone, shouldn't I put my house, stock, and bank accounts in joint tenancy with my children?*

or

> *I want my favorite niece to have my four-plex when I die. Shouldn't I put it in joint tenancy now with her?*

Generally, the answer to both questions is no, for at least five reasons:

1. You might expose the property to attachment or attack in case a judgment is taken against any of the children—or the niece.
2. If a child or if the niece should die before you do, the property would have to be cleared by you, at a cost.
3. You may run into a gift tax problem.
4. You may change your mind and want a different arrangement later on. But all joint tenants must agree before you can have your property back. Sometimes one or more can't —or won't.
5. There are better ways to accomplish what you want, such as by Revocable Trust and other ways set forth in detail in this book.

(See Chapter 11, "Avoiding Probate Through Use of Joint Tenancy.")

## When You Are No Longer Able

These three similar inquiries came from the same seminar:

*When I'm old and can't handle my own affairs or take care of myself, what are my options?*

*Is a power of attorney a good thing?*

*What's the difference between a power of attorney and a conservator?*

When a person is incapable of managing his or her property or personal affairs, as determined by a Court of Law a *Conservator, Guardian,* or *Committee* is appointed by the Court to assist and protect that person.

Where permitted by law, as in California, a person may nominate a Conservator, but though the Court will usually abide by the nominations, it is the Court's right to appoint in the best interest of the Conservatee (person needing help).

A *Power of Attorney* is a revocable instrument in writing, whereby a person gives another person power to act on the giver's behalf. The power can be *special* (that is, power to do a specific act or acts) or *general* (that is, power to act in a broad, general way on behalf of the one giving the power).

In some states the power terminates or ends at the death and, in some states, incompetency of the giver. Some states permit the power to continue even if the giver becomes incompetent or dies, and this is sometimes called the *durable power of attorney*.

With human rights getting ever-increasing attention in the courts, and the court procedures involving conservatorships and guardianships getting progressively more burdensome, many are deciding in favor of a *trust* to accomplish all of the above, with the trustee empowered to act on behalf of the person who needs help.

Options you can consider with your attorney, then, are:

1. The Power of Attorney;
2. A Conservatorship, or other court-appointed vehicle;
3. Joint Tenancy, say, with a relative or friend;
4. A revocable or irrevocable living trust;
5. Complete care facilities which may utilize one or more of the above.

*How can my Social Security checks be cashed if
I can't sign my own name?*

The Social Security Administration has a relatively simple
procedure they use to solve this problem. Please call their
local office for this advice.

*If I become incompetent, is my will still valid?*

If you were competent at the time you executed your will,
later incompetency does not affect the validity of the will.

*I have no living spouse and no children. I want
my house, furniture, and savings to go to a
Christian organization when I die. How can I
best accomplish this to avoid expenses at my
death?*

I'd recommend a revocable trust. (See Chapter 12, "Avoid
Probate Through the Living Trust.")

*My spouse has died. I have four savings ac-
counts, live in a rented mobile home, and have
a little furniture. I want my estate to go to four
charities. How can I do this without probate?*

You can use the Totten or Bank Trust or other living trust
arrangement with the bank accounts, and a living trust with
the remaining property. (Refer to the Index for more information on these various trusts.)

*I'm leaving $2,000 to each of my grand-
children. What's the best way to do this?*

If you need use of all of your funds for as long as you live,
then you can give these sums through your will, or by use of
the Totten Trust. If you don't need the money, you might
consider making a gift of it now so as to get these funds out
of your estate for tax and/or probate purposes. You can give
$10,000 or less per person per year without any gift tax and
reduce your estate by the amount of the gift.

## If It Has Happened to You

The funeral, crowds, cards of sympathy, casseroles from the neighbors and church ladies—all are a part of the past now. Friends and relatives have gone back to living their own lives and you are alone. Aside from the fact that you have many business affairs to put in order, now you must face a different type of life than you've ever known before. We would like to suggest a few things that have proven to be a lifeline to many who have gone through what you are experiencing.

## First and Foremost

1. *Get your life spiritually in tune with God.*

The Bible says, " . . . these are written, that you might believe that Jesus is the Christ, the Son of God; and that believing you might have life through His name."

Jesus said, " . . . I am come that they might have life, and that they might have it more abundantly." Life *abundant—eternally* and *now*—even in your aloneness. He will give you direction, purpose, and peace if you surrender your life to Him. It is His promise: "I will not leave you comfortless . . . . "

Your Bible needs to come off that shelf and receive constant attention from you. In it is a remedy for every sorrow you have.

You need to spend time with our Lord in prayer—continually.

You need to spend time with others who share your faith. And that brings us to our next point.

2. *Don't wallow in self-pity.*

Some seem to enjoy playing the martyr. They are happiest when they think others are feeling sorry for them. But that's a miserable way to live a life. So you've lost a loved one! It's true that you have a right to grieve. Even Jesus wept at the death of a friend. But life is to go on! Fall and winter are just a prelude to spring and a new life. Your loved one wouldn't want you to sorrow unduly.

Martha Snell Nicholson expressed it so well in this lovely poem:

## For You

The things you loved I have not laid away
To molder in the darkness, year by year;
The songs you sang, the books you read each day
Are all about me, intimate and dear.

   I do not keep your chair a thing apart,
   Lonely and empty—desolate to view—
   But if one comes a-weary, sick at heart—
   I seat him there and comfort him for you.

I do not go apart in grief and weep,
For I have known your tenderness and care.
Such memories are joys, that we may keep
And so I pray for those whose lives are bare.

   I may not daily go and scatter flowers
   Where you are sleeping 'neath the sun and dew—
   But if one lies in pain through weary hours
   I send the flowers there, dear heart, for you.

Life claims our best, you would not have me waste
A single day in selfish idle woe,
I fancy that I hear you bid me haste
Lest I should sadly falter as I go.

   Perchance so much that now seems incomplete
   Was left for me in my poor way to do,
   And I shall love to tell you when we meet—
   That I have done your errands, dear, for you.

3. *Think spring!*

Plan a cruise or do something you've always wanted to do but couldn't. Tear yourself away from endless hours in front of the TV. Update your wardrobe! Take a charm course!

4. *Take stock!*

Where do your abilities lie? In what direction do your interests move? Start to carve out a new life—perhaps a new career. Remember, this is the first day of the beginning of the rest of your life.

5. *Consider important decisions.*

Now may be the time for you to go into a business deal or invest some money. Be sure you do these things with the guidance of professionals in each field. It is best to choose these people from among those you know or have had dealings with in the past, or with whom your friends have had good dealings.

6. *Get involved in the lives of others.*

Some people, especially if they are older, will say, "I don't really have any friends," or, "People don't like me." Remember, to have friends you must *be* a friend. Don't force yourself into lives where you don't fit. But there are always those who NEED your friendship. If you feel others don't like you, take a good look at yourself.

> Uncle Frank was cranky, ornery, touchy, critical, and always complaining that "People never ask me over or come to see me." Everyone blamed his disposition on the shock of losing his wife, Martha.

The truth of the matter was, Uncle Frank was just what he had spent years in becoming. The reason people didn't notice it, and overlooked his crustiness, was because Aunt Martha was always so sparkling and charming!

You may have formed some very unpleasant personality traits as years went by. You may need to take a course on how to win friends and influence people. For beginners, you might try a course the Bible offers. The first lesson starts with I Corinthians, Chapter 13, in the New Testament.

Then as soon as you've conquered YOURSELF, or even if you haven't quite reached that lofty goal, you can reach out to others who need your love. Do volunteer work in some organization; work for your church; get involved in the missionary society; visit rest homes; bake pies for the neighbors; make friends with neighborhood youngsters or teenagers who need someone with whom they can just "talk"; adopt a child through a service agency, such as World Vision, whose children are in foreign countries. We know of single people who have done this, and have had the joy of traveling across the ocean to visit their orphans. (See page 101.)

Keep in mind: Everybody needs somebody. You be the somebody someone needs—now.

7. *Be careful when it comes to affairs of the heart.*

A very difficult part of being alone is being without the one with whom you had a vibrant, satisfying, physical relationship. Widowers often find another mate before long, but as mentioned before, there are over ten million widows needing someone to love them. Many of those widows would like to remarry.

In fact, a show of any affection from the opposite sex will rekindle fires of emotional need that can spell trouble for the unwary.

One woman called while we were working on this book. She'd had a very good marriage previously, but had lost her husband in death. Then she met another fellow who had been married and divorced three times (which should have told her *something).* He abused her and then left her

for yet another woman. She is in a deep state of depression
and is going to a psychologist for help.

She would have been wise to have had this man checked
out by a discreet detective before she married him. Before
*you* get involved with a new partner, be sure you know him or
her well. It might be wise to have an antenuptial agreement
drawn up, including your desires regarding your property.

And be realistic.

> Mary, a widow who was sixty-three years old, was not
> very attractive. However, she was extremely intelligent and
> taught school in a college.
>
> She became good friends with a young man, thirty years
> her junior. They enjoyed many hours talking and sharing
> their academic interests. She became very emotionally at-
> tached to him and felt he must be in love with her.
>
> Imagine her shock when he happily announced to her
> one morning that he had found his true love and would be
> married soon. He had looked upon her only as he would a
> substitute mother. Romantic involvement was the last
> thing on his mind.

In the marriage seminars Margaret and I conduct across
the nation, we usually have a group of singles who attend. In
our question/answer periods with them, we have come to the
conclusion that most single women, whether they've never
been married, or are divorced, or widowed, are nearly con-
sumed with the idea that they *must* get married! Such an at-
titude is almost guaranteed to chase men away, not bring
them around! If you are busy doing fascinating, exciting
things, you won't be dwelling on the desire to be remarried
which can lead you into foolish decisions.

**Sexual Traps**

There's a real danger of falling into a sexual trap when you
are lonely. Some counselors say, "Do what you think is best.
If it feels good, do it! Morality is a matter of one's conscience. And conscience is dictated by your upbringing which is
often erroneous!"

I'm very grateful that God has not left us to cap the volcano of physical desire alone. God's rule for the uncertain teens, the single person, and everyone else has not changed. God invented sex, but he placed certain boundaries around its use, for OUR good, not His.

Sex works for your benefit and the benefit of your partner, IN a marriage relationship, not outside of it. God isn't like some mean old man keeping candy from a baby. He knows fire is great in the fireplace, but it causes a lot of trouble when it burns in the middle of the living room floor.

**Chapter 17**

# *What Actually Takes Place When I Die?*

In a few cases, I suppose, there will be rejoicing. As one tombstone of times past records it: *I put my wife beneath this stone, for her repose and for my own.*

In most instances, however, there will be someone mourning the fact that you have gone. In fact, the death of a loved one can be the most traumatic experience of a person's life. Sometimes the need to tend to many details accompanying that death reduces the trauma somewhat, not giving the grieving person too much time for sorrow.

### I've Been Asked

> *Do you think I should have detailed burial and funeral instructions for my loved ones to follow after my death?*

If you wish, but accomplish what you want with a minimum of detail. Circumstances change from day to day and too many instructions may place a burden you wouldn't want your loved ones to bear.

A person can leave written instructions concerning the funeral on a separate sheet of paper or include it in his or her will. These instructions are to be followed, subject only to some restrictions of local law, even though the will has not been admitted to probate.

I PUT MY WIFE BENEATH THIS STONE FOR HER REPOSE AND FOR MY OWN...

If the person leaves no instructions and a family dispute arises over some details of the funeral, the law usually resolves the dispute by giving the right to decide to designated persons, starting with the surviving spouse. However, this is normally a time when families can and do agree.

Some people even prearrange and pay for their funeral, but most leave this to be done for them. Whether prearrangements are made or not, the representatives of the funeral home or mortuary are always extremely helpful. They'll remind those involved with the arrangements for the need of giving notice to the newspaper, advising relatives and friends, ordering flowers, arranging for the service, ordering death certificates, applying for Social Security and Veterans' Administration death benefits, acknowledging gifts of flowers, and so forth.

> *What are the minimal requirements for disposal of a body so as to keep expenses down when a mortician may be trying to "sell a job"?*

Local health and safety laws place certain restrictions on what can be done with a body. Check your local law.

## Once a Funeral Is Over

The survivors may need help obtaining and processing a myriad of forms pertaining to benefits due the decedent and the estate. This help can come from an experienced relative, friend, or from your attorney.

Then it must be determined whether the decedent "just let it happen," as we wrote about in Chapter 5; planned ahead and included probate, as we explained in Chapters 8 and 9; or planned ahead and avoided probate as discussed in Chapters 10 through 13. The survivors must act accordingly. Hopefully, plans were made by the decedent so that settling his or her affairs can be an orderly and relatively painless process.

### *Who takes care of paying bills?*

Your estate is liable for your bills and funeral costs. It may be that an executor, administrator, or trustee will pay your bills, depending on what arrangements you have made, or if your estate has none of these, then it may be a surviving spouse or relative who does the job.

Generally, if a will is involved, the attorney who drew it up is called by one of the survivors, and the team of executor and attorney goes to work. If the executor is inexperienced, the attorney must spend time educating and instructing the executor, but in any event they accomplish the following:

> Take steps to safeguard the assets of the estate;
> Offer the will for probate;
> Collect and inventory all assets and have them appraised;
> See that the estate is administered;
> Have the taxes determined;
> See that claims are settled and debts are paid.

The executor then prepares and submits an accounting to the Court, has it approved, and distributes the estate as directed in the will of the decedent.

### *Upon my death, can my spouse get the will*

### *from the safe deposit box?*

Yes, if the bank (or other depository where the box is located) and the law in your state allow it. Check with your depository for any possible restrictions. (See the section entitled, "Where Should Our Wills Be Kept?" in Chapter 6.)

### *Must my property be sold and divided up?*

That will depend upon whether there is sufficient cash available in your estate to pay your bills and other costs of winding up your affairs. If there is sufficient cash, then the property can be distributed in kind (that is, intact, or as is, without sale).

There are situations where there has not been sufficient cash to pay bills and costs, and relatives or friends wanted specific property, so have advanced cash to the estate, in order that bills and costs could be paid and the property could be distributed to them.

One such case involved the family home which was left to three adult children. One wanted the home, so purchased the interest of his brothers for cash, which cash he borrowed on the house from the bank.

### *If I have a going business, must it stop on my death?*

Not immediately, and, of course, not at all if you have arranged for someone to continue the business. Special instructions concerning the operation and disposition of the business can be included in a living trust, or in your will. If no other arrangements have been made, the executor can keep it going just as you would have and then dispose of it so as to best settle your estate.

### *If I give my house to someone in my will, and I have a loan on it secured by a mortgage, who pays the loan?*

If your will is silent on the question, then the person takes the house, subject to the loan. If you want the person to take the house debt-free, then state that in your will and specify that the debt is to be paid out of a certain fund you provide or out of the residue of your estate.

### What happens to my minor children immediately after my death?

If your spouse, who is also the children's parent, survives you, then that parent will be responsible for the care of your children. If there is no surviving parent, then the Court must appoint a guardian of the persons, and, if any estate, for the estate of the children.

Usually children stay with relatives or friends. Where no relatives or friends are available, they are placed in a juvenile facility and then in a foster home as soon as possible.

You have a right to nominate a guardian in your will. The Court rarely decides against your wishes, and only when the judge believes someone else could better serve the children's interests in this capacity.

### What is a living will and should I make one?

Modern machines are available to keep your body functioning artificially long after chance of recovery is gone. A living will is the title given a document directed to your doctor, family, and others, wherein you request that you be allowed to die and not be kept alive by artificial means, if there is no reasonable expectation that you will recover. Laws have been passed in some states recognizing this as a right of an individual, in one degree or another. Most states, however, do not recognize this as an enforceable right, but rather look on it as a statement of your desire, which may or may not be followed.

But be careful. I know one couple who signed living wills. The wife contracted a sickness which required artificial help to keep her from dying. Because of her living will, she was not given this artificial help and passed away. Now, several years later, the husband lives with the nagging thought, "Would she be alive and with me today if she'd had help?"

He'll never know.

*We suggest:* that if you want a living will for yourself, you might consider requesting the machines be turned off only after you have had help, say, for a month or so, after reasonable expectation of recovery is gone. But give the machines some time. Many people are alive and well today because of machines.

### When I die I want my body used for science. How can I see that this is done?

The Uniform Anatomical Gift Act is in force in most states in response to the need of medical science for the human body and its parts, and in response to a desire of people to serve others.

You should make contact with a medical school, hospital, or doctor near you. They will assist or advise you as to completing the necessary arrangements.

### There Are Even More Important Things

It's one thing to leave this earth's scene and not have to answer for what is going on in your absence. It's another thing altogether to find that your life has NOT ended, that you are faced with eternity, and to realize that SOME of the decisions you made while still alive in the flesh are going to affect what's going to happen to you now. Since those decisions, and especially one of them, are more important than anything we have discussed in this book so far, let's consider that next.

# Chapter 18

# *It's Up To You*

On one of our tours to the east coast, Margaret and I had so many pieces of luggage and electronic equipment, and so many boxes of books and records, that we sent a number of them ahead to arrive at various destinations where we would be holding seminars and concerts. Had we overlooked any of them, we would have found ourselves in a very uncomfortable position, for our tightly planned schedule left no time for emergencies!

Although it is true you can't take anything with you when you leave this earth, you can " . . . lay up . . . treasures in heaven . . . ." while you are still on the earth—sending them ahead, so to speak.

This is done in many ways, including using your material possessions to further God's kingdom, bringing freedom, hope, joy, peace, physical comfort, and the opportunity for eternal life to those in need. In this volume, we have discussed how you can use your will, trusts, and other ways to accomplish that goal. But you needn't wait until death to put your money to work. You can open the strings on your purse and let the money flow out where it will do the most good. Remember the promise, "Bring ye all the tithes into the storehouse, that there may be meat in mine house, and prove me now herewith, saith the Lord of hosts, if I will not open you the windows of heaven, and pour you out a blessing, that there shall not be room enough to receive it."

God never fails to keep His promise, if we keep our end of the bargain. A tithe is 10 percent of everything we make. God has allowed us to use the other 90 percent for ourselves. But those who have learned that EVERYTHING they have belongs to God, and they are merely stewards of it, have learned a very important lesson indeed. Those who give 15 percent, 20 percent, 30 percent, or more of what they earn have discovered riches beyond measure.

### The Bigger Shovel

A man of moderate income was asked, "How can you give so much money to your church? You have a family to support!"

The generous giver replied, "I guess it's like this: I shovel in . . . the Lord shovels back to me. And *His* shovel is bigger than mine!"

### The Widow's Mite

In the Scriptures, we are told of a widow who gave her last penny to the Lord's work. Jesus commended her greatly. A banker estimated that, if that widow's mite had been deposited in the First Citizen's Bank of Jerusalem to draw 4 percent interest semiannually, the fund today would total $4,800,000,000,000,000,000,000.

If a bank on earth could multiply the widow's mite to such an astronomical figure, think what treasures such a dedicated person would have awaiting her in heaven, for God's counting goes beyond the known.

The tithe, leaving money to the Lord's work through our wills, trusts, and in many other ways, as discussed in this volume, will continue to bring freedom, hope, joy, peace, material comfort, and the opportunity for eternal life to those in need.

### What will happen to my estate in the event of The Rapture?

There's a very interesting parallel between the law and God's Word regarding missing persons. For those of you who aren't sure what The Rapture is, let's take just a moment to explain it. The word *Rapture* does not appear in the Bible, but has come to be accepted as the description of events as set forth in I Thessalonians 4:16-18 where the dead and living in Christ will be caught up into the air and away from the earth:

> For the Lord himself will come down from heaven with a mighty shout and with the soul-stirring cry of the archangel and the great trumpet-call of God. And the believers who are dead will be the first to rise to meet the Lord. Then we who are still alive and remain on the earth will be caught up with them in the clouds to meet the Lord in the air and remain with him forever. So comfort and encourage each other with this news.

Many believe that the Bible teaches that a period of *seven* years will pass following the above described event (The Rapture), during which time certain horrible happenings, known as The Great Tribulation, will take place here on the earth, as vividly described in the Book of the Revelation in the Bible. At the end of this time, Christ intervenes at the Battle of Armageddon and returns to the earth in power, accompanied by Christians who have been away with Christ for those *seven* years.

**The Law Says**

When a person has disappeared and the person's whereabouts is unknown for *seven* years, that person legally is presumed dead, and the Court will issue letters of administration for disposing of the person's property. This presumption of death after *seven* years' absence exists in a majority of the states in our United States as a common law or statutory rule of evidence, though some state legislatures have changed the period.

*American Jurisprudence,* 2d Edition, says that the presumption arising from *seven* years of unexplained absence is based in the United States on English common law and is generally, if not universally, followed for all legal purposes. This is true except where it has been changed by statute. So, we might speculate: At the end of the seven years' period, just about the time the officials are ready to dispose of the missing Christians' properties, *back* they come, very much alive. Interesting thought, isn't it?

**One More Decision to Make!**

Often, after I have helped a client plan an estate, and the will and/or trust has been drawn up, witnessed, and signed, I ask, *Now that you've made provision for your material possessions and what will happen to them after your death, what have you done to make provision for your soul? Are you ready to meet God!*

I receive various answers. Many people haven't the foggiest notion. They've spent a lifetime acquiring, satisfying the flesh, and preparing for old age, but have shut the spiritual out of their lives or have never gotten down to business with their Creator.

They are like the young athlete who wanted to participate in the Olympics. He practiced hours each day on his skill, shopped for clothes, packed his suitcase, wrote letters, attended parties in his honor, bought airline tickets, and finally arrived where the Olympics were to be held. But no one could find his name in the list of registered participants. He had failed to realize that there were certain rules he was supposed to follow in order to be accepted and allowed to compete. He lost out completely as a result.

So it will be with multitudes who have counted this brief life on earth more important than preparing for eternal life the way our Heavenly Father has told us to do. Jesus said, " . . . strait is the gate, and narrow is the way, which leadeth unto life, and few there be that find it." And He spoke directly to all those who have pinned their hopes for security on material possessions, "For what shall it profit a man, if he shall gain the whole world, and lose his own soul?"

There are many ways people rationalize the whole situation rather than coming to grips with the issue. Among them are the following:

The atheist says, "I don't believe in God." But the Bible answers: **The fool hath said in his heart, there is no God . . . .**

The unknowledgeable states, "There are many ways to God. All sincere people will make it to heaven someday." But God silences that argument with: **There is a way which seemeth right unto a man, but the end thereof are the ways of death.**

"I'm not so bad," states the self-righteous. "When God weighs the bad I've done against the good, He'll let me in." But the Bible disagrees and tells us: **. . . we are all as an unclean thing, and all our righteousnesses are as filthy rags . . . .**

"I don't have to think of that for a long time. I'm too busy," retorts the busy person. That's what a certain rich man said, but God said to him: **Thou fool, this night thy soul shall be required of thee: then whose shall those things be, which thou has provided?**

Once a neighbor called me in his usual inebriated state and hiccuped into the telephone, "Mishter Hardisty? I'm sh-sh-shellin' my propitty." He sloshed on, "Wouldja like to buy it?"

My mind was on other things, finances were rather low, I wasn't sure he knew what he was doing, and I didn't really want to *think* about buying property right then.

I quickly answered, "No, thanks, Mr. Ennis. I'm really not interested."

I made the wrong decision. The property doubled in price soon after he sold it to someone else. Many a fortune has been missed by someone making the wrong decision.

Make sure you don't miss the greatest fortune of all! Take time to THINK this business of eternity through carefully.

Happily enough, making peace with your Creator and obtaining the gift of salvation from Him is not as difficult as some would have you believe. But just as you must make provisions for what will happen to your estate in the event of your death, according to the law, so you must make provision for the salvation of your soul according to the way God has set forth.

Jesus said, "I am the way, the truth, and the life: no man cometh unto the Father, but by me." He also said, "Ye must be born again."

The process of being born again is a spiritual one, not physical. When you recognize that Jesus is the ONLY way, and realize WHO He is, you can only cry out to God for mercy, knowing that the sinless Jesus died to bear the punishment for the things you have done that offend God. When you do this, the sincere desire to be forgiven and to start life anew with God in control is tenderly and graciously acknowledged by our Lord. In that moment, a personal relationship with Him begins. He, in the form of His Holy Spirit, enters your life and your name is written in the Book of Life in heaven, never to be erased. You become His child! Born again! Not into man's family, this time, but into God's family.

When He takes residence with us, He brings a trunk full of promises. Those promises, available to any child of God *as he meets the conditions accompanying those promises,* are such things as: peace of heart and mind (which the rich would like to buy, but can't); a certainty of eternal life (sought for by mankind since the beginning of time); joy (a scarce commodity these days); a desire to live righteously; help in trouble; and countless other blessings worth more than millions of dollars in blue-chip stock.

Furthermore, our Heavenly Father has written our names in His heavenly will, promising those of us who have received His Son an inheritance that encompasses riches beyond our imagination. They are described in part like this:

> . . . Eye hath not seen, nor ear heard, neither have entered into the heart of man, the things which God hath prepared for them that love him.

After studying in seven different colleges and universities and sitting under the tutoring of some of the world's greatest philosophers, I am more convinced than ever that if *anyone* would examine the evidence—scientific, archaeological, circumstantial, historical, and that found in the changed lives of untold numbers of men and women—he or she could only come to the conclusion that the Bible is truly God's written word to us.

(For books that present such evidence, please refer to our Bibliography.)

Why not surrender your life to this One who loves you so much? Why continue to serve the one who delights in exalting fame, fortune, immorality, self, and the other things that are responsible for bringing misery and sorrow to this earth? You have that decision to make. It's up to you.

# Scripture References

All references are based on the King James Version of the Bible, unless otherwise noted.

# Bibliography

American Law Institute-American Bar Association Committee on Continuing Professional Education: *Estate Planning in Depth.* 2 vols. Philadelphia, Pennsylvania, 1982.

Annual Institute on Estate Planning, University of Miami, Matthew Bender, New York, New York.

California Continuing Education of the Bar, Impact of the Economic Recovery Tax Act of 1981 on Estate Planning and Administration, Berkeley, California, 1982.

Casner, A. James, *Estate Planning,* 6 vols. with 1982 supplement, Little, Brown and Co., Boston, Massachusetts.

Commerce Clearing House, Inc., *Tax Reform Act of 1969,* Chicago, Illinois, 1969.

Commerce Clearing House, Inc., *Technical Corrections Act of 1982,* Chicago, Illinois, 1983.

*Estate and Gift Tax Changes Under 1976 Tax Reform,* C. C. H. Editorial Staff Publication, Commerce Clearing House, Inc., Chicago, Illinois, 1976.

*The Estate Planner's Complete Guide and Workbook,* Panel Publishers, Inc., Greenvale, New York, 1982.

Estate Planning Research Group, Ltd., *Estate Planning Quarterly,* Tampa, Florida, 1983.

Kess, Sidney; Westlin, Bertil; and Whitman, Robert; *Financial and Estate Planner,* Commerce Clearing House, Inc., Chicago, Illinois, 1981.

Practicing Law Institute, Tax Law and Estate Planning Service, New York, New York, 1983.

The Research Institute of America, Inc., *Estate Planning and Taxation Coordinator,* 7 vols., New York, New York, 1983.

The Research Institute of America, Inc., *Federal Tax Coordinator,* 28 vols., New York, New York. 1983.

*Taxwise Giving,* 2 vols., Conrad Teitell, Old Greenwich, Connecticut, 1983.

## BOOKS ON FINANCE

Bowman, George M., *How to Succeed With Your Money,* Moody Press, Chicago, Illinois, 1979.

Burkett, Larry, *Your Finances in Changing Times, Christian Financial Concept Series, Revised,* Moody Press, Chicago, IL 1982.

Fooshee, George, Jr., *You Can Beat the Money Squeeze,* Fleming H. Revell, Old Tappan, New Jersey, 1980.

Lucky, Camilla D., *You Can Live on Half Your Income,* Zondervan Publishing House, Grand Rapids, Michigan, 1982.

Metz, Robert, *Future Stocks, Investing for Profit in Growth Stocks of the 1980's,* Harper & Row Publishers, New York, New York, 1982.

Nickerson, William, *How I Turned $1000 Into Five Million in Real Estate,* Simon & Schuster, Revised Edition, New York, New York, 1980.

Porter, Sylvia, *Sylvia Porter's New Money Book for the 80's,* Doubleday & Company, Inc., Garden City, New York, 1979.

Randle, Paul A., and Swenson, Philip, *Personal Financial Planning for Executives,* Lifetime Learning, Division of Wadsworth, Inc., Belmont, California.

Taylor, A. H., and Pocock, M. A., *Handbook of Financial Planning and Control,* Renouf USA, Inc., Old Post Road, Brookfield Vermont, 1981.

## BOOKS REGARDING BIBLE AUTHENTICITY

Criswell, W. A., *Why I Preach That the Bible is Literally True,* Broadman Press, N. Nashville, Tennessee, 1969.

Henry, Carl F. H., *God, Revelation, and Authority,* Word Books Publishers, Waco, Texas, 1976 (vols. 1 & 2), 1979 (vols. 3 & 4).

Lindsell, Harold, *The Battle for the Bible,* Zondervan Publishing House, Grand Rapids, Michigan, 1976.

McDowell, Josh, *Evidence That Demands a Verdict,* Revised Edition, McDowell Publishers, 1979.

Rademacher, Earl D., Editor, *Can We Trust the Bible?, Leading Theologians Speak Out on Biblical Inerrancy,* Tyndale House Publishers, Inc., Wheaton, Illinois, 1981.

Ryrie, Charles, *We Believe in Biblical Inerrancy,* Walterick Publishers, Kansas City, Kansas, 1980.

Unger, Merrill F., *Archaeology and the New Testament,* Zondervan Publishing House, Grand Rapids, Michigan, 1979.

# Index